This book belongs to

THE 10 MINUTE FIX

100 SIMPLE WAYS TO FEEL BETTER NOW

CATHERINE GREER

Balmoral Press

BALMORAL PRESS

balmoralpress.com.au

A catalogue record for this book is available from the National Library of Australia.

ISBN (print): 978-0-6488471-0-6

ISBN (Kindle): 978-0-6488471-1-3

ISBN (Apple iBooks): 978-0-6488471-2-0

ISBN (audiobook): 978-0-6488471-3-7

Cover design by KW Creative

Author photograph © Merilyn Beretta

For corporate or bulk sales, please contact sales@balmoralpress.com.au

Balmoral Press

For my mom, Katie —
the original Catherine Greer,
and the one who loves yellow.

~

Why is yellow important?
You'll find out in Chapter 64.

CONTENTS

INTRODUCTION

I believe so many things can be fixed in ten minutes. Sounds crazy, but it's true: a tough task, a bad mood, a sour conversation, a dirty floor, flossing, even a workout—ten minutes and done. My ten minute theory is why I wrote this book.

I guess you could call me an Instant Gratification person. If I can have it now, start it now, do it now, I will. Even if it's hard, I feel so much better when I dive in. I'm a do-er and I love being in control.

Then COVID-19 changed the world.

Our lives got smaller, people we loved got sick, far too many suffered, and our daily routines shrank to the size of our homes and balconies (if we were lucky). When my world got smaller, that was a big problem. Why? Well, here are a few more things you should know about me: I'm an author, a copywriter, a blogger at LoveOurAge.com, a wife and a mum. I cook, walk the dog, love to bake and yes, I argue regularly with my teens. I'm a productive, busy adult —like you. But I'm also claustrophobic, especially in small airplanes and elevators, and it's getting worse as I get older.

The idea of my world *shrinking* was not good for me.

COVID felt like an invitation to live in a closet. And don't even get me started about being marooned on this beautiful island of Australia, unable to get back to Canada, my first home.

I was struggling. So I took a deep breath, carried a coffee and my laptop into our backyard in Sydney and started writing. I had one goal: to make *myself* feel better now.

You see, I already knew all 100 of the fixes that made it into this book—but I was forgetting to *use them*. I needed an easy reference guide for my own bedside table, a quick read with all the good ideas in one easy place.

"If I write it down," I thought, *"I'll remember what to do."*

How to use *The 10 Minute Fix*

Every idea in this book is practical and do-able. I believe we need simple ways to feel better *now* because *now* is where we live. Not in the future. Not in the past.

- **Read from start to finish**—and be encouraged to begin again or try something new.
- **Dip into any chapter**—and find a 10 Minute Fix that's practical and helpful.
- **Write down your thoughts**—there's space to explore the ideas you love.

I hope *The 10 Minute Fix* becomes your reminder that you're doing better than you think you are, and it's going to be okay.

1

THE 10 MINUTE FIX

Let's kick off by talking about avoiding stuff. Do you tend to avoid a tough job that needs to be done, or is this only me? I needed to wash off the pendant light hanging outside on our patio, covered in winter grime. I hate that job. I hate cleaning.

Enter the 10 Minute Fix.

Here's how I motivate myself: I set the oven timer for 10 minutes. I promise I'll clean until it goes off. Grab the bucket, fill with hot water and soap, drop in a cloth, wipe the pendant lamp. It's messy and slimy, but I keep going. Back into the water again, and again, then once more until I finish. Surprisingly, I have time to spare, so I sweep under the table, get rid of cobwebs, swipe my cloth over the messy barbecue.

Beep beep. Time's up. And it's done.

Why is it so hard to remember that most tough jobs take 10 minutes?

Seriously, what if we did 10 minutes of exercise right now? Squats and push-ups, my friend, for 10 minutes. Or how about this: 10 minutes of meditation. 10 minutes of stretching. 10 minutes of working on your book. De-cluttering. Cleaning your cutlery drawer.

It always surprises me how much I can get done in 10 minutes.

The 10 Minute Fix

Choose the thing.
Set your timer for 10.
Do.

2

WHAT ARE YOUR QUIRKY BITS?

Here's a story for you. Yesterday, walking the dog in our suburb of Sydney, my husband and I explored a grassy laneway between two houses, and we came across the most beautiful scotch thistles.

Weeds. Truly pretty weeds.

My husband waited while I found a way to break off the thistles, then he made an invention with dog bags so I could carry the weeds home. It worked perfectly: a dog bag 'strap' to carry prickly thistles for over a kilometre back to the house.

That's him. That's me.

Ingenious helper. Gatherer of beautiful weeds.

We are who we are.

It made me think of a famous quote my son has on the wall behind his desk. It was written by Thoreau, an American author, philosopher and Transcendentalist who lived in the mid-nineteenth century. Thoreau was a naturalist who spent two years living at Walden Pond, and famously published the book *Walden*. It defined his life.

Here's the quotation—you've probably seen it before.

Most men lead lives
of quiet desperation,
and go to the grave
with the song
still in them.

So many people read this Thoreau quote and assume they haven't done their thing.

I think we can't *stop* ourselves from doing it. Our song leaks out. It's who we are.

Not many people would notice weeds in a laneway. Not many people would find them pretty. Almost no one would write about them and think the message was worthy to put in a little book and send around the world.

I'm not saying I'm so special. Please don't get me wrong. There are so many things I don't see at all: science (blah!) or babies (ugh). Swimming...nope! Not my song. Maybe it's yours. But there's this: somehow, seeing what's 'pretty' in the world makes me *me*.

Victoria, a beautiful friend with a wise heart, told me this story a few days ago about her unexpected chance to speak at an open mic in a cafe last year. She's a talented actor but she got too mixed up about perfection and she let the chance pass her by.

Then Vic felt terrible. And she said this:

I knew I should have done it. My mama raised me better than that.

4
———

MISTAKES

Yes, I've made a few and some were terrible. Here's a quick but honest list: I had an early, short and disastrous failed marriage that I'm not proud of and never talk about. It took me more than fifteen years to love the country I immigrated to, and even longer to understand its people. I regularly teach rather than mother my sons, and have set impossibly high standards for them at certain points in their young lives. These mistakes and many more make me cringe when I think about them.

I know you have your own list of mistakes, too.

We don't discuss our mistakes much, especially when they cause us pain; instead, we live around them like sand in an oyster.

But we have a choice.

The trick is to transform the sand into a pearl.

How? The only way I've found to do this is to consider my mistakes with curiosity instead of shame.

- Who was I when I acted this way?
- What did I believe or not know at all?

Put it first in your day, and it will get done.

Because here's the truth: the emails, the kitchen, the dog, your workplace—all of that is another person's priority, not yours. That's the world asking you to put its needs first. Yes, it's important. But so are you.

> If you want to move the dial on your own life, you have to work on your goal as if it's the most important thing.
>> Do your thing first.

That's how I wrote my books. That's how I'm writing this one now.

Like your life, mine is busy: work, family, lots of house-work, shopping, cleaning, laundry, gardening, side hustles in copywriting. But if I want to get the new book written, it has to come first.

A page a day for 365 days is a book. A workout a day for 365 days is a fit body.

Can you put your dream first?

Please say *yes*.

3

MOVE THE DIAL TOWARDS YOUR
DREAMS

D o you know how to move the dial towards your dreams? I've been thinking about this a lot lately —about how to do all the things I have to do, and still prioritise what will get me closer to my goals.

Why is working on our dreams so hard to do?

Honestly, I don't think it's an issue of self-esteem so much as it's an issue of practicality. We know we matter, and we know our dreams and goals matter, too. But often we do all the small tasks first (clean up the kitchen, answer the emails, make that phone call, walk the dog and on and on it goes) and we promise ourselves this: *Once I take care of these urgent things—once I clear some space for myself—I'll sit down and do the thing that's important for me.*

We wait to:

- Research the new job opportunity.
- Write the book.
- Exercise.
- Write the song lyrics.
- Explore the business idea.

Today, please sing your kind of song.

Inventor of solutions or finder of beauty? A person who always helps a child? A heart that wants to problem-solve? Baker or walker? Kitchen dancer?

Let it out. Appreciate it: the quirky, beautiful person your mama raised you to be.

You are irreplaceable.

∾

Three Things That Make You "You"

1. ....

2. ....

3. ....

∾

If we can learn from our mistakes, then we can grow around them. We can share life lessons with each other. Then do this:

> Forgive ourselves for not knowing better. Or for knowing better but not doing better.
>
> And move on.

You're doing the best you can today, and you'll do better tomorrow. So will I.

~

Here's The Truth

It's likely that *you* are the only person
thinking about your mistake right now.
You can choose to stop reliving it.
You can decide to move on.

~

BE GENTLE WITH PEOPLE

There's a drawing I love by Steph Ferrell that summarises human relationships beautifully. You can follow Steph's work at decade2doodles.com or find her on Instagram @decade2doodles.

The gist of Steph's drawing is this: if you drew a line from one side of this page to the other, and then highlighted the last centimetre at the end using a blue highlighter, the black line would represent a person's life. The blue bit at the end would be what you know about it. Almost nothing.

This is true for every single one of us: we know so little of what is going on in someone else's life—even if we love them.

True about me.

True about you.

That's why we should be gentle with people.

Our minds want to fill in the blanks and make up a story that makes sense about somebody else, but we just don't know what's going on for anyone, not really.

So today, no stories. No filling in the blanks. No assumptions. Make a decision to be gentle with people—and with yourself.

Send some peace around the world right now.

Remember the tiny blue highlighted line? Remember the much longer black one?

It doesn't matter what the circumstance is, or who did what. We only know a little bit of what's going on.

ROUGH EDGES

My favourite quote in the world is actually something my older son said when he was fifteen. We were having a fight involving me correcting some aspect of his behaviour—his manners, his attitude, something about him I thought just wasn't right and didn't measure up.

And he said this:

My rough edges are my best part.

The self-knowledge in those words made me stop, mid-correction. Because he was right and I was wrong. Our rough edges make us who we are, and often point us in the direction of our true north.

Argumentative? Maybe you're meant to stand up for people. Sad or anxious? Maybe you're sensitive to the deeper things in the world that not everyone sees. A rule breaker or a rule follower? Maybe you value freedom or believe strongly in justice. Overly talkative? Maybe you're someone who is hungry to learn.

We all have what other people would call rough edges—but are they there for a reason?

And when we get attacked about our behaviour or character or some aspect of who we are, like I so unfairly confronted my son, it's important to remember this: we have rough edges, but we are not the problem. The problem is the problem. And we have time to sort it out.

∾

You Are Not The Problem

The *problem*
is the
problem.
Your rough edges
may be your best part.

∾

SWITCH YOUR BUFFER

I wonder what you do when you're stressed and how you've learned to manage it. The truth is, most of us (probably all of us) 'buffer' against bad feelings. I first heard about this term from Brooke Castillo, owner of thelifecoachschool.com. If you haven't listened to Brooke's podcast, The Life Coach School, I highly recommend it.

Buffering means we find a way not to feel. We numb ourselves. It looks like this. I'm upset so I...

- Overdrink
- Find the chocolate
- Tell the same story over and over

I have one weird buffer I'd add to that list: I walk.

All my life, since I was a little girl, my buffer has been walking. As a child growing up on a farm in the Canadian prairies, I walked for miles in the fields and country lanes. In boarding school, I walked city streets. When I moved across the country for grad school, I did relentless daily loops around a city park. When I immigrated to Australia, same thing: I have walked every suburb we've lived in. I do it still. Honestly, I don't even do it for exercise. I do it because it helps me process.

So, here's my thought—can you make a buffer switch? Drinking wine becomes drawing, chocolate becomes walking, over-Netflix watching becomes watching YouTube videos about things you want to learn. I think the key might be what you did or loved as a child.

We all buffer, and we all need to learn to go through the bad feeling from start to finish, and not push it away. But in the meantime, while we're learning to face our feelings, maybe a buffer switch can help.

- Switch in strawberries for chocolate.
- Switch in soda in a pretty glass for wine.
- Switch in walking for telling the same story, over and over...

A switch is a good place to start.

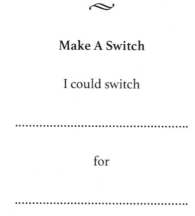

Make A Switch

I could switch

....

for

....

ARE YOU LUCKY?

About a year ago, Jules, a favourite friend of mine and an author at JulesVanMil.com, gave me the best advice I'd ever heard—and she didn't even know it. She told me a story about her grandmother who, of all amazing things, actually played and won the lottery! And Jules concluded her story with a line I will never forget:

My grandmother always said she was born lucky.

That phrase stuck with me, and I decided right then and there, at fifty years old, that I was born lucky too.

I whisper this to myself all the time, over issues big and small.

Silly, right? But actually, very helpful.

When something great happens, I remind myself that I was born lucky.

When I'm worried, I tell myself that I was born lucky—and that everything will be okay in the end.

My life hasn't always been easy, far from it.

But here's the truth: if we're able to read this book, we are born lucky.

We have so much: somewhere to live, clean water and friends. Most of us have family or people to love.

Considering ourselves lucky is being grateful for every good thing, and even the smallest things are good.

My husband, who served in the Royal Canadian Navy and the Royal Australian Navy, always says to me, "If no one is shooting at me, it's a good day." He's joking, of course, but that's true perspective, isn't it?

I was born lucky.

You were, too.

NO B.S.

I spend a lot of time walking and thinking, dreaming up ideas for new novels, and just figuring out what I want to do with the last half of my life: years 50 to 100. This week, I was listening to a podcast while I walked, and Lisa Bilyeu said something I loved. When starting a new project or tackling a challenge, she asks an important question:

No B.S. What would it take to do this?

The part that got me is "No B.S." Because if you're even a bit like I am, you spend at least a little time B.S.-ing yourself about what you're going to do before you actually DO IT.

- No B.S. What would it take to work full time and write a book?
- No B.S. What would it take to start a side hustle?
- No B.S. What would it take to improve my health?

Such a great question. It flips my mind over into solution mode, rather than staying stuck in the problem or the endless possibilities. It has a way of making us put the chips down and ask, realistically, what it would take to start.

Now's a great time to lay aside our own B.S. and start a list. Writing things down is the first step.

～

What Would It Take?

I've always wanted to

....

No B.S.—what would I have to do
to move closer to this goal?
(Or give up? Or learn? Or become?)

1. ....

2. ....

3. ....

4. ....

5. ....

～

10

THE BEST RELATIONSHIP ADVICE

I t's just one simple phrase—and the best relationship advice I know. In fact, this might be the most important 10 Minute Fix in the whole book. From three tiny words, you can instantly improve your:

- Friendships
- Partnerships
- Romance
- Parenting

It doesn't matter how bad things have become, or how many mistakes you've made. It's not patronising, and it won't cause someone to feel you're employing a weird psychological trick. Just say these three simple words:

Tell me more.

Then listen. *Tell me more* gives breathing room to the people we love. Try it with someone (anyone) today and you'll see what I mean.

DRAGONS AND DESTINY

My friend, Sharon, invited me to a party. Think beautiful dresses, candles, jazz, the dark sea stretching ahead of us, a balcony set for sixty people, wine and laughter.

It was so much fun. And something amazing happened. Sharon leaned toward me, with absolute confidence, and told me that someone she loved was overseas.

"He's off slaying dragons," she said. "But he'll be home soon."

I can't describe what I learned in that moment, but I want to try. Because all of us—every single one—we all have dragons.

Mine are probably different from yours.

Maybe it's confidence, and you need more but you don't know where you're going to get it. Or a tough time at work. Kids you love who are breaking your heart with their sadness. Someone is unwell. Maybe that 'someone' is you.

Money dragons.

Fear dragons.

Dragons of desire for something you can't have, and the dragon is eating you up with worry and need.

I decided, in that moment at Sharon's party, that I would think of myself as a dragon slayer.

Strong.

Brave.

Alive.

I want to live from a place of courage and strength. I want to choose the kind of person I'll be...no matter what life hands me.

We can't control the dragons. But this week, we can decide to go off and try to slay them. And come back home soon.

~

Slaying Dragons

What dragon do you need to slay?

....

~

12

PAPER TOWEL PEOPLE

A while ago I had the privilege to listen to Tiffany Aliche (thebudgetnistablog.com) on a podcast, and she mentioned three words that really stuck with me. So smart. Incredibly wise. Are you ready?

Paper Towel People. I'm paraphrasing roughly here, but Tiffany said something like this:

> When things go wrong, some people are worriers or shouters or blamers. And some people just grab the paper towels.

So true. Whether it's a tiny, literal problem—the kid has written on the walls AGAIN—or something much bigger, we have two choices. Freak out or grab the paper towels.

The truth is that we can't fix anything when we sit in the problem. We have to switch our brains into solution mode. If we can do this quickly, the quicker the better, we can get to the other side and solve what's wrong.

As a writer, I am truly great at imagining all sorts of scenarios and playing them out in my mind as if they are real. It's a fabulous quality when you're writing books, but a little less fabulous when you're in relationships.

I'm dramatic. My brain loves to worry and stew. So I'm trying to switch over to being a Paper Towel Person. Calm, solution-focused, ready to act...not speculate or inflame. It's hard work, but it's worth it. And yes, all my relationships— being a mum and being married—are so much better because of it.

∿

What About You?

Paper Towel Person or not (yet)?
It's worth considering
for the sake of all the people we love.

∿

13

IT'S NOT A DUMB IDEA

If you've been in my kitchen or follow me on Instagram, you've seen this: a framed print of my favourite stanza from Wallace Stevens' lovely poem, "Thirteen Ways of Looking At A Blackbird."

> I was of three minds
>   like a tree
>   in which there are three blackbirds.

I love how Wallace Stevens twists the cliché and makes a beautiful, new truth.

I don't know how you're travelling, but lately I've been of three minds...wondering what writing project I should start now, wondering where to go from here.

Because isn't this the truth?

Everything we want requires us to grow.

It's outside our comfort zone. And it's far too easy to become paralysed by confusion.

So, what do we do?

We follow people who seem to know it all, and who can do it all. We consume information and compare ourselves with experts on Instagram and Facebook, or the friends we know in real life who have already done it. We watch other people and it seems easy for them, and sometimes we feel like we're falling behind.

But like I tell my writing students over and over: you can only learn to do a thing by doing it. You teach yourself, one step at a time.

Because this is also the truth.

Whatever it is, whatever you're dreaming about learning or doing...it's not a dumb idea. It's YOUR idea.

Time to start.

Have some fun outside your comfort zone. That's where I'm heading.

∼

Get *Out* Of The Zone

What's one thing you've always wanted to do
that's outside your comfort zone?

....

∼

HAPPY THANK YOU MORE PLEASE

Wow. I love this phrase so much that I wear it on a t-shirt. It sums up my attitude to life. In fact, I think we should say 'Happy, Thank You, More Please' about all the tiny miracles we get to enjoy.

- I got to hold the sweetest baby girl last night at dinner.
- I made a truly delicious papaya chicken salad for some people I love.
- In my local park, I chatted with three women I admire.

And there's so much more: lilies leftover from my birthday perfuming the entire room, a birthday card resting on the piano, (a piano! a miracle!), a full clean dishwasher, the carpet vacuumed, sunshine, a sleeping dog who loves our family. I have a laptop. My fingers can type. The coffee is hot. A friend sent an email that she loved my novel.

And yet—you know this, too: I could give you a list of the other sort.

I could just as easily tell you that there are always bills, that I have a stressful meeting at work on Monday morning, that I can't run anymore because my foot is permanently injured. That I missed out on a job I wanted. That I'm worried. Sad. Unsure. All of it. But I choose to say Thank You. I choose to give attention to what I want to grow in my life—and that tiny shift in attitude has served me so well.

Wherever you are right now, and whatever you're facing, I hope you take a moment to enjoy your day. Thank you for all you do. Thank you, world, for offering a series of tiny miracles for us to appreciate. Happy. Thank You. More, please. It's my mantra. Join me.

～

Would You Wear This Shirt?

Want to order a *Happy Thank You More Please* t-shirt? Let me know at catherine@loveourage.com

～

GOOD NEWS, BAD NEWS

Recently I read a hilarious quote by Sam Lamott (at hellohumans.co) that sums up everything I've learned about life in the last fifty years. When I read it, I laughed out loud.

The good news: you're a hero!
The bad news: you have to save yourself.

If you were here with me right now (in pjs, with a morning coffee) while everyone in my house is still asleep, I would tell you this: you're going to make a wonderful hero.

All that hard work that seems to be for nothing?

The trying and falling short?

The worry that you're not enough—not good enough, smart enough, talented enough, hard-working enough, pretty enough, young enough, fit enough?

You're doing better than you think you are.

Sometimes, my friend, you just have to keep going. Yes, the cavalry is coming...but it's you.

We are our own heroes.

So we have to be there for ourselves. We have to catch ourselves when we're falling. And then we have to do this: keep going.

Be Your Own Hero

From me to you, right now:
You're doing better than you think you are.
A lot better.

16

THE BEST QUESTION

S ometimes I have found myself in a metaphorical tailspin, overthinking everything and feeling stuck. Worrying. Replaying all the worst possible scenarios and every stupid thing I've ever done or said.

Are you the same?

Here's what I learned from my American friend, Kristen, and I thought it might help you, too. When times are tough, Kristen told me, this is the best question to ask ourselves:

What is the gift?

- When you're worried about something, what is the gift?
- When your kid is in pain, what is the gift?
- When you've been disappointed, what is the gift?

I should tattoo this on my wrist. It's such a great question. It always helps me get myself back on track.

If you're feeling a little down (or worse), if something has happened that's frightening you, if you have a deep worry you haven't shared with anyone, I hope it helps you, too.

What Is The Gift?

What is your current worry?

....

What is the gift inside this problem?

....

17

SLOW DOWN YOUR YES

You'll know this if you're a friend of mine in real life: I am (mostly) a Yes Girl. I will take it on, make the leap, give it a try, have a go. Often I will be obliging and do what others want me to do, just because I like to be nice. I'm also a hard worker, so this means I have a huge capacity to help out.

So I do and I do and I do until...I get tired.

What about you? Are you any good at saying no?

I believe most of the time our fear makes us say NO far too often. And truly, every single one of my blessings has come about when I've done things I was scared to do.

- Write a book.
- Immigrate to Australia.
- Get married.
- Change careers.

Yes, yes, yes, yes.

On the other side of every scared YES, I've always found a bigger, stronger, more capable version of myself. Saying

YES has been good for me. I have dozens of examples to prove it—everything from teaching an online writing course to doing a bit of modelling to being a guest on several podcasts to taking on tricky finance writing jobs.

But I know that this is also true:

Sometimes it's best to slow down your yes.
Sometimes it's right to say NO.

If you're feeling a little tired, maybe it's time for a break. Maybe it's time for a NO to everyone else, so you can say YES to yourself.

18

WHAT DO YOU DO FOR FUN?

A few months ago, I went to a function on a Thursday night that was filled with bankers and insurance people. Though the view was fabulous —overlooking Sydney Harbour—let me be honest: the event had the potential to be fairly dry. We were there because of work, after all.

That's why I decided to try something new. I can't remember where I read this tip!

Instead of chatting with people about work, I asked this... "So, what do you do for fun?"

And it was amazing.

At first, every single person thought I'd asked them about work. They answered about their current job title and position, and I had to say, "No, no...I asked what you do for FUN!"

Suddenly, people were talking about surfing, or how they're learning adult ballet, or how they want to have more fun in their lives but aren't sure what they love to do. We were loud and we were laughing.

And the weird thing was this: any time a new person

wandered over to our group, someone said, "Oh, we're just talking about what we do for fun." (Like...aren't we cool? We talk about FUN.)

It makes me think this: wow, we are missing out.

Too busy.

Too serious.

We forget that we can choose to enjoy ourselves.

Even if you have to work today, I'm sure there's some time, even fifteen minutes, for some fun.

Have you thought about it? Or are you always mired in the serious, the productive? Maybe it's time to rediscover what lights you up a little.

~

Do You *Know* What You Find Fun?

(Not what you *think* you should find fun, but what is truly fun for you? For example, people say travel is fun...but I don't love it. I love to cook an elaborate family dinner, or learn the secret to baking perfect French macarons.)

What is fun for you?

1. ....

2. ....

3. ....

~

19

PLAYING BIG AND PLAYING SMALL

I think a lot about playing big and playing small, especially since I achieved my dream of publishing a novel in 2019 with Penguin Books. It's a Young Adult novel called *Love Lie Repeat*, a thriller about the pressure to be perfect and strained relationships between mothers and daughters. If you're interested, you can find it anywhere books are sold.

Since I published *Love Lie Repeat*, everyone is allowed to have a public opinion of my writing. Some people love my book and have written glowing reviews. Some don't. Some have made valid points about what I could have done better. Some people have been critical and, quite frankly, unkind.

It all happens in public, for everyone to see and comment on.

Can you imagine that?

Getting a 3-star rating when you speak at a meeting?

Getting 5-stars for your dinner party, or 2-stars for your parenting? And it's out there, in public for everyone to see, forever? Whew!

But my feeling is this: I'm a beginner, and I'm doing the

best I can. So here's what I'm learning in my fifties, my friends!

It's time to grow and let my life get bigger.

It's scary, but it's also time.

Just asking...is it time for you to get bigger, too?

Are you with me? Let's not apologise for the size of anything.

- Our bodies.
- Our needs.
- Our dreams.
- Our attempts, which are definitely not going to be perfect.

This year, let's not spend a single second being quiet so we don't irritate people. Let's not match the size of our lives to the size of someone else's expectations of us.

And even if there's criticism (especially when there's criticism!), let's keep going.

Let's continue to shine.

20

BEAUTIFUL, NOT PERFECT

Could this be your time to start something new? One of my favourite quotes from artist Morgan Harper Nichols (at morganharpernichols.com) is about our creativity:

> This is the season she will make beautiful things.
>
> Not perfect things, but honest things that speak to who she is and who she is called to be.

I love Morgan's idea of making beautiful things, not perfect things. What would happen if we decided to stop trying to be so perfect? Maybe it's time to be free from the tyranny of doing it right all the time.

We could:

- Be a beginner.
- Start something.
- Try what we're afraid to attempt.
- Admit that we've got a dream.

We could be producers, not consumers.

We could be cheerleaders—not critics—of other people who are busy creating.

They are not perfect. Neither are we. None of us have to be, and that's a beautiful relief.

Start Small

What would you like to create?

....

Can you start small,
and let yourself be imperfect?

EASE UP

Hey, hard worker, I see you. Just for today, stop blaming yourself for things you didn't get done. Life is twisty and some things take time; we don't always know why events unfold as they do.

My wish for you right now is this...

Slow down.

Enjoy.

Breathe in, then out. We often breathe so shallowly.

It's okay to take your time. It's okay to let things unfold.

～

How To Relax (even at your desk):

1. Take slow, full breaths.
2. Massage your own hands.
3. Flex your wrists, clench your fists and release.
4. Gaze across the room, far into the distance.

～

YOUR TO DON'T LIST

I heard about this idea from American blogger and author, Erin Loechner, whose writing and work you can find at designformankind.com. I truly love Erin's perspective and her thoughts on living a deliberately slow, contemplative life.

Erin says that for everyone with big To Do lists, it's good to have a healthy To Don't List, too.

What's on your To Don't List? Have you ever thought about it?

Okay, I'm getting real here. My short list:

- I don't colour my hair anymore.
- I don't rehearse and replay mistakes from the past.
- I don't race around in the morning. I always have coffee first, and think quietly about my day.
- I don't spend time with people I don't admire.

Your To Don't list is important for your mental health.

Have you ever given yourself the freedom to make one? I hadn't, until Erin inspired me.

Who are you, and what *doesn't* matter to you?

What Don't You Do?

What isn't worth it, to you?
To Don't List:

I. ....

2. ....

3. ....

4. ....

5. ....

HOW TO SOLVE OVERWHELM

Whenever I feel overwhelmed, I do this simple 10 Minute Fix. I'm almost embarrassed to share it because it's so basic, but it helps me every time. Maybe it will also help you.

I keep a block of A3 paper on hand (the big one, the size of two sheets of regular paper), and whenever I feel stressed and overwhelmed, I grab a sheet and a sharpie. I write the year in a heart in the middle of the page. Then I brain dump everything that's waging war in my head onto the page. I usually chunk out my thoughts by month or by category, arranged around the page.

My categories might be:

- Writing
- Work
- Family
- Books
- Blog
- Health

Or my categories might be more specific, for example:

- Love Our Age website strategy
- Gifts to buy
- New book ideas
- House repair jobs

I make it as visual as I can, a mind map. My one piece of paper solution has become my go-to coping mechanism. (So much healthier than chocolate, right?)

One big piece of paper, with everything on it.

Sometimes I stick the page up on my wall in the study, replacing as I write new ones. Sometimes I just look at everything in one spot, and then I transfer jobs to To Do lists (or To Don't lists). Sometimes I stare at the sheet and breathe and remind myself that it's do-able and not as jumbled and overwhelming as I thought.

Why does it work?

There's magic (for me!) in the relief of putting everything in one place, outside myself, and in seeing it visually at one time...not in a series of lists down a page. Maybe it will also work for you.

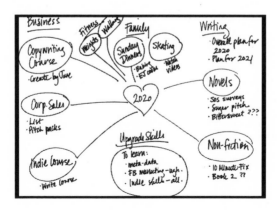

SLOWING DOWN WILL SPEED YOU UP

O ur world has a time-famine mindset. Time flies. It's scarce. We need more time. Faster is better, right? But sometimes faster is just faster. Sometimes slower gives us all the energy we need to figure out the right solution to a problem or the best way forward.

It's not how most people think.

The world is filled with hustle, my friends. But it should also be filled with some days that are deliberate and slow.

Here's to slowing down today. Deep breaths, sip your coffee, smile at the people you love.

~

Go Slow

Do your best to slow down
and listen to every story you're told.

~

WHAT I'D TELL MY YOUNGER SELF

I f I could tell Young Me one thing, it would be this. (Actually, I'd tell her to go put on sunscreen...and then I'd tell her this.)

Everyone is a Russian doll, a matryoshka.

Weird, right? But we are. We hold every version of ourselves that we've ever been, and the trick is to let ourselves—and other people—grow.

Try, fail, change, grow.

Forgive, love, keep going, expand.

We don't have to peel back layers to get to some true 'unchanging' self. We add layers on.

We iterate.

We grow larger and become new (and hopefully wiser) versions of ourselves as we age. Every human on the planet has the right to say this:

That was then, and this is now.

If we can let go of old stories, if we can stop holding people hostage to versions of themselves that they used to be, then we can all be free.

I'm so curious to know if you agree. Would you say that you've iterated into the person you are now?

Have you given yourself the gift of forgiveness for being younger and not knowing better?

∾

What Would You Tell Your Younger Self?

1. ....

2. ....

3. ....

∾

26

WHAT EVERYONE WANTS

D o you know what everyone wants? Everyone wants to be seen—really seen—by you. They want to know they are enough for you, just as they are, without having to improve or be a different version of themselves.

The meta message behind everything we say is this:

Do you see me?

One of the most humbling experiences I've had as a mother happened when my younger son was eight years old. We were talking about the sport he would choose at school during winter term, and he couldn't decide which suited him best: basketball or soccer. I casually said, "It doesn't matter. You like both, and I wouldn't change a thing about you."

That last line stopped him in his tracks. He flung his skinny arms around me. I could see in his little face how much my words mattered. And I realised I should be showing him a lot more often that I meant what I said.

I wouldn't change a thing about you.

What a powerful sentence. If someone feels appreciated and loved by you, it's because when you look at them, you take time to actually see them.

Seeing someone means removing your story about them. It means accepting them in their human imperfection and loving them anyway. When we don't require or ask people to change, they feel free to be themselves.

Everyone is so hungry for true love.

True love is just this: being seen—really seen—by other people.

～

True Love

Here's what I'm going to try:
deep breath,
see the person in front of me,
love,
repeat.

～

27

MARRIAGE S.O.S.

Just keeping it real: can we talk about screens? And relationships? Do you ever feel like your conversations are split between a human and what's on your phone or theirs? My husband and I are a busy couple, and it's hard to admit that there are days and days when our marriage looks like screen plus screen. Two laptops. Two coffees. Two people. Two phones.

We're all facing the same question, right? How much is too much? When do the screens intrude and stop us from talking to each other?

We check them so often. Email, Instagram, Facebook. Too often.

BF Skinner, behavioural scientist, discovered that to ingrain a habit, you give rewards at variable times in variable sizes. The lab rat knows it'll be given food for pressing the lever, but not exactly when or how much.

The result? A compulsive rat.

It's exactly the same with humans. Variable intermittent reinforcement explains why we hang around waiting for those hearts in Instagram and Likes on Facebook. We check-check-check and keep checking.

What are we looking for? Love on a screen. Notifications that tell us we matter. A dopamine hit. Chemical affection.

I had an epiphany while I was sleepless at 4am, and it was this: for the next while, I'm going to look for love in real life.

It's an experiment.

I'm looking for human connection, for "variable intermittent reinforcement" from a chat with a stranger in the fruit and veg market, from unexpected teenage hugs from my boys, from a wink from the guy I married twenty years ago.

If you need a little relationship S.O.S. (and I know that I do!), maybe try this: *see* the person in front of you and step away from the screens, especially around the people you love.

∾

7 Fun Love Hacks

1. Sit side by side at the table, not across from.
2. Walk your neighbourhood together at twilight.
3. Celebrate a small victory.
4. Argue as if you're a neutral third party and you want the best for both of you.
5. Hold your partner's hand.
6. Leave a tiny treat beside their keys.
7. Ask openly for what you want.

∾

28

HOW WOULD YOU DO IT?

I love to consider this simple question from Australian entrepreneur and author of *Earth is Hiring*, Peta Kelly. If you're interested, you can find Peta on Instagram @petajean_ Her question is deceptively straightforward, but very smart:

> If you didn't know how it should be done,
>
> how would you do it?

It's a fun idea to think about. How would YOU write a book, or plan a kitchen renovation, or meditate? How would YOU throw your ideal party, or run a company?

It seems like common wisdom to "be yourself." We tell kids this all the time. But sometimes we get a little unclear on what this actually means. Instead of being who we are, we want to get straight to the good stuff—success. This can translate into believing we should be like other people, the ones who are successful and, therefore, 'doing things right.'

Almost two years ago, I read a question and it stopped me cold. It was this:

> If you could be the woman of your dreams,
>> who would you be?

That question made me start writing. I answered it by admitting my dream: I would be a novelist and a non-fiction author.

Am I perfect? *No.*

Does everyone love my books? *No.*

Do I do it all 'right'? *No.*

Am I as successful as J.K Rowling? *Well, I wish. But no.*

Despite all that, I got started, and I'm doing things how I do them. It has to be enough, for me and for you.

So, here's to your dreams.

How would *you* do it?

How *will* you do it?

About Your Dreams

> If you could be the person of your dreams,
>> who would you be?

....

> What would you do?

....

> (Yes, often our dreams are side hustles,
>> and that's perfectly okay.)

29

"I APPRECIATE YOU"

For the early years of this marriage, I was a military spouse. My husband served as a Navigator first in the Royal Canadian Navy, and then in the Royal Australian Navy. During those years, especially when we immigrated to Australia and I knew not a soul, I learned to love and trust my husband when he was on deployment for months and I was alone. It was pre-Facetime. It was *hard*.

That's when I started using three little words that meant so much to our marriage. I don't know any words more powerful. They deliver what every person—partner, child, friend, colleague, family member—needs.

I appreciate you.

When I live by these words, and appreciate everyone around me, I watch people bloom. If you need to spruce up your relationships, try it. "I appreciate you" and "Tell me more" are the two best ways to say I love you.

In fact, I believe they're better than "I love you."

Try it and see if you agree.

30

IS IT TIME TO DOUBLE DOWN?

R ight now in my world, it's time for me to Double Down. What this means is that it's time to get cracking and get some work done.

I have great stuff going on, and problems going on, and my floors are perpetually dirty and I need to get my dental check-up. And there's laundry and broken tiles at the front door and a dog that needs walking every single day. And there's exercise to do and shopping (how can teenage boys eat SO MUCH so often?) and friends to grab a coffee with, and kids to chat with when they're worried.

In other words, my life is like your life: good stuff, fun stuff, hard stuff...lots of stuff!

So instead of freaking out, I'm going to Double Down. In this season of busy, I'm going to get productive. I'm going to find more hours in my day, get up that bit earlier, work later and Get. Things. Done.

Because, truly, I'm happy. I'm happy that I have a lot going on. I'm happy even for the challenges. The challenges are life. It's such a whopping big cliché, but it's true:

These are *our* good old days, problems and all.

If we're honest, we all have more time in our twenty-four hours than we think we do.

(But this is also true: if you're tired, please allow yourself to rest. Double Down if it's time for that.)

∼

5 Top Productivity Tips

1. Clear your clutter.
2. Do. (Don't think so much!)
3. Cut to the chase.
4. Stop consuming information. Start creating.
5. Bad day? Press re-set. Shake it off physically, like animals do.

∼

31

HEY, DROP THAT CHEW TOY

We tell a story about everything. Often, we forget that we have the ability to choose: are we telling a good story or a bad one? Helpful, or not? (And maybe the most revealing question of all: do our stories have a central theme? For example, is it always someone else's fault? Are things always going wrong?)

We have control over how we experience our worlds, but sometimes we hold onto a story like a dog with a chew toy. Have you been there?

Will. Not. Let. It. Go.

But here's the thing. It's possible that the stories we're telling are wrong.

My friend, Jess Lively (at jesslively.com), host of The Lively Show and believer in going with the flow, made me laugh when I was complaining.

"Can you just drop the chew toy?" she said. "Can you let that one go?"

It's all a story. Everything.

We don't have the imprimatur of "reality" or "the truth" on our side. We see things a certain way and we judge, but we don't know for sure. We definitely don't know all the details.

We can't see inside another person's heart. That's why I'm asking myself more often:

Can you drop that chew toy?

It makes life so much easier.

~

Time To Make A Change

Recurring problem?
Opinion that isn't helpful?
Constantly complaining about the same old thing?
Maybe it's time to drop it,
pick a better story to tell, and move on.

~

32

ARE YOU ON YOUR OWN SIDE?

I magine me, age 11. I had a pink coat I loved. It was a spring jacket and it had a photograph of a kitten on the back, in 1970s fuzzy soft-focus. Yep, truly! That coat was everything to me, especially since—with six kids in our family—we didn't get new clothes often. I loved it with my whole heart.

But one of the girls in my little country school didn't like me, so every morning I'd walk down the lane to wait for the bus, and I'd take off my pink jacket and fold it up inside out so that when I got to school I wouldn't trigger her anger.

Back then, bullying was handled in kid-to-kid combat. Remember those days? It didn't occur to me to confront her. I was too young to understand that her life wasn't happy. Instead, I told myself a story that went like this: *there must be something wrong with me. I have to hide what I love. It's better when I blend in.*

I wasn't on my own side. (Not back then.) But now I am. Are you?

Some of you will be rolling your eyes and thinking, of course I am!

But for some of us, it's a confronting question. Do you tell people, honestly, what you love? Do you stick up for YOU? Do you embrace and honour all the versions of yourself, throughout your life...at 11 and 27 and 50 and 70 and 90? Both your goodness, and your mistakes?

It's taken me a long time, but in my 50s I won't take my jacket off and hide for anybody. I am who I am and the people who love me will find me.

I hope you feel the same about you.

Now that I'm older and wiser, I realise (of course!) that the little girl who "hated" my jacket probably desperately wanted her own pink kitten coat and someone to watch over her. We never truly know what's going on with another person (and sometimes, in retrospect, we don't even understand what we were thinking. Or doing.)

That's why I hope you're kind and gentle with all the versions of you that you've been.

I hope you're on your own side.

33

YOU ARE TOO MUCH

A story for you. I had a boyfriend in university, a drummer in a band called The Rhythm Pigs, whose mother really loved me. She was a teacher and made the most delicious Greek lemon chicken. When I broke up with her son, she cried and hand delivered the largest bouquet of pink tulips. My next boyfriend had a mother who didn't love me; she had a curly perm (it was the 80s) and made comments like, "Catherine, you wear your heart on your sleeve." Her face was always sour when she said my name.

Which woman was right?

They both were.

I am not for everyone. Neither are you. And that's why our job in this life is to run toward the people who "get" us and give a happy wave goodbye to the people who don't.

It's what bestselling American author Glennon Doyle says (at momastery.com):

You will be too much for some people.

They aren't your people.

People will tell you that you're too loud. Or too introverted. Or too serious. Or maybe they just won't know what to do with you in general.

But here's the thing: we've been put on this planet to express ourselves. To BE ourselves. If that means writing your truth and kitchen dancing and hugging your teenagers and loving your dog as if she's a person and wearing hot pink and going grey and being effusive and wearing your heart on your sleeve...that is okay.

You are meant to show up as you.

I'm going to show up as me.

When we find our people, it's like fireworks and magic. We all know this feeling.

But here's a question: what do we do with the people who don't love us (or who we don't love)? I use a visualisation trick I learned a long time ago. See if it works for you!

∾

The Boat Exercise

Imagine putting that person in a boat
and pushing the boat out to sea,
far, far away from you.
Wave goodbye, turn around and walk towards
the people you love.

∾

34

FILL UP YOUR CUP

Question for you: what makes you love your Saturday? For me, it's writing for you or my future novel readers, then coffee with my husband, saying goodbye to a teenager who is able to drive himself to sport (it's the best when they get their driver's licence...DO NOT BE AFRAID! REJOICE!), an afternoon with a friend at a fashion event I'd never go to on my own.

Fun, rest, peace, beauty.

I've been thinking about this a lot lately: what fills up your cup?

Do you know your answer?

Because often we fill up with stuff we don't love.

I used to fill up with a lot of quick fixes or unhealthy defaults. Things like (so obvious!):

- Chocolate
- Mindless scrolling
- Worry
- Avoidance

My mind would zoom from "I feel tired" to "Here, this will fill the emptiness" without even thinking whether the "this" was what I really wanted.

Our brains crave familiarity: good or bad, it doesn't matter. That's why, in the last year, I've thought about good ways to fill my cup. I'm embarrassed to share because some of these things may seem lame to you, but here we go:

- Find something beautiful to look at.
- Take a photo.
- Stretch, right where I am.
- Sip black coffee—extra hot, but not too strong.
- Make a promise to myself and keep it.
- Walk around my back garden and listen to a favourite song on Spotify.

Even now, I struggle to list more healthy things that fill me up...but I love the idea that my list is growing.

So here's a hug and a question: do you know what fills up your cup? Rest, rest, rest...refill.

~

What Fills Up Your Cup?

1. ....

2. ....

3. ....

~

35

INDULGING IN CONFUSION

L ately I've been thinking honestly about indulging in confusion. Brooke Castillo, founder of The Life Coach School (at thelifecoachschool.com) introduced me to this concept and she's absolutely right. You can listen to Brooke discuss the idea on The Life Coach School Podcast.

It's a great word: indulge.

We indulge in confusion when we allow ourselves to say "I don't know how to..." Our confusion gives us a tidy excuse to stop. After all, we don't know how to write a book, start a podcast, sew a dress, travel solo, start a business.

We're confused.

It's hard.

Toooooooo hard.

If you're like me, you might tread water a while in that murky space in your brain.

The problem is this: when I indulge in confusion, I stay stuck. Let me give you an example or two. Lately, I've been confused about these things:

- Should I resurrect, revise, update and relaunch my online course, How To Write Your Book This Year? Will I offer the online class to all my blog readers? Will it take too much of my own writing time? *Confusion*.
- Should I get a foot operation in the hopes that I can run again? Do I want weeks on the couch? Will my foot be worse after surgery than it is now? *Confusion*.
- I love Sydney. I love Canada. We're citizens of both countries. Do we move after our son graduates? Where will our boys end up living? Do I have the energy to move again? *Confusion*.
- I love writing non-fiction. I also love writing novels, though it is definitely harder to do. Am I meant to do both, or just do what comes easiest? *Confusion*.

And there I balance: generally happy, generally productive, but indulging in confusion.

Are you with me? Do you ever say, "I don't know how to do..." and stop yourself from moving forward?

It's true that we need to show up before we're ready. We can figure out most things. And we all know that learning makes us feel fantastic and being a beginner is okay.

Here's my promise: the next time I indulge in confusion, I'm going to

- Act.
- Try something.
- Figure it out as I land.
- See what wonderful things Life has to throw in my direction.

Succeed (I hope), fail sometimes, have fun doing all of it.

Ready, Steady, Go

Maybe it's time to jump in and decide.
What are you indulging in confusion about?

....

HOW TO WIN

Of course, everyone wants to win. We want to win someone's heart, or maybe win the lottery, we want to win the regatta or the basketball game, we want to win the 'good looks jackpot' or win the business deal or the contract, or just win in life.

But often we don't.

So does that mean we lose?

As I was thinking about winning and losing, I decided this:

We should call it winning or learning.

Because truly, learning is all we ever do if we have a forgiving attitude. We can afford to be kind to ourselves. Who else will do it if we don't?

Kindness. Let's try that today.

TRY ADDING, NOT SUBTRACTING

C ould we try adding, not subtracting this year? Instead of stopping things (like bad habits) can we think about adding in better ones? Together, collectively, can we decide to go BIG?

I know that sometimes the world wants us to be small.

Quiet.

Pleasing.

I know that sometimes we want to 'get healthy' and be physically smaller. But even if it's time for you (like it is for me) to take gentler care of our faithful, hardworking bodies, can we think about body-care as adding, not subtracting?

Can we think, I'm adding in:

- More water
- More greens
- More sleep
- More positive comments about myself

Maybe it's time to expand and say this:

I'm going to add more love into my life—for everyone and for me.

Add In

What easy things can you add into your life?

1 ....

2. ....

3. ....

4. ....

5. ....

38

YOU LOOK GOOD WHEN YOU'RE TIRED

This week came as a big surprise: I got sick, and I never get sick. Nothing serious, but there it was, and it lasted quite a few days and it really knocked me over.

I'm so used to barrelling forward and being, you know, a hard worker. I want to be inspiring; I want people to know I'm here, cheering for them from the sidelines. Plus, I like to make things as stress-free as I can for our kids, especially during exam week. I drive. I pack healthy lunches. But suddenly, this week, I just couldn't do it. Everything ached: head, body, even my dreams ached.

Being sick reminded me of this:

Everyone has their own true story, the story we don't often tell.

We're good at showing up in full armour, in full make-up, with our hair done and our teeth whitened. What we're not good at is sharing when we feel small, less than, beleaguered by life.

This week has truly made me wonder: where do we get the idea that we're not allowed to take a break, or stumble, or be tired? Whatever makes us think we have to be strong all the time?

Funny thing is, I wouldn't expect that from anyone else. Neither would you. We would both rush in with soup and sympathy.

If you're feeling tired today, my lovely friend, I have this to offer you. Exhale. Let your shoulders relax.

You look *good* when you're tired. You look like you could keep on going...sometimes it's a badge of honour, and it's beautiful.

39

WHAT ABOUT YOUR PAST? AND MINE?

A couple of years ago I was visiting my beautiful high school friend, Heather, in Canada. We were strolling through a balmy, mozzie-filled Saskatoon evening when we turned a corner and literally walked into the quarterback of our high school football team.

You guys, I went from 50 to 15 in about three seconds flat. So did he.

It was weird. I definitely wasn't flirting and neither was The Quarterback. Still, I could feel all the years fall away in one big WHOOOOOSH and there we were, back in high school. Except we were 50.

Have you ever had this happen?

For me, I carry the little girl who loved to read, the high school cheerleader (Go, Lions!), the grad student with her cool jeans and serious novels (Go, Mustangs!), the young English teacher, the exhausted mummy overseas raising babies, the copywriter and business owner and now the novelist and non-fiction author.

Sure, I look 50. But I feel every age I've ever been.

Do you feel that way, too?

All the versions of ourselves that we carry can get heavy. It's tempting to pretend that we never were that person, or made those choices, or ran full steam ahead into those traps. But we are, and we did.

In the past, I used to want to ditch a few Previous Catherines (permed hair and leg warmers, anyone? Or much worse, the woman who made some serious mistakes and hurt other people and herself) but now I believe it's important to embrace every one.

That's why I decided to take a deep breath.

I gathered all the versions of myself together in my mind and I had a little talk with all those Catherines.

I told them I finally understood *why* they acted the way they did.

And now, when I think of my past, I do this:

I feel the things I don't want to feel.

I feel them and forgive myself.

I allow myself to be free.

Accepting all the versions of ourselves (young and older, light and dark), sprinkling a lot of compassion and heading back to self-love—that's what I do now.

I hope you do, too.

40

HOW TO FIND WHAT LIGHTS YOU UP

M y mom is Catherine Greer (the First), called Katie or Kate by family and friends. She's 87 and lives in Canada. One Christmas a couple of years ago, I sent her a ukulele.

It was love at first sight.

She'd never had the opportunity to be a musician, but she raised us singing. As the youngest of six kids, I spent a lot of time picking raspberries and singing all the songs my Mom loved (*Five foot two, eyes of blue...Oh what those five feet can do!*).

Mom visited me last year in Sydney, and she's now pretty accomplished at playing her ukulele. One day, we had a conversation:

Me: "When did you start playing, Mom? Were you 84?"
   Mom: "Oh no! I was only 83."

After she started lessons, my Mom joined a group called The Ukuladies. These women completely rock. Beth, their musical director, is in her 80s, and at one time they had a 91 year old playing electric guitar. They range in age from 60 to 90+ and, when they're able, they perform for other seniors in their city.

Let me say this: when I think of my mom and her friends, I think of women like me, with a few decades more life experience. They're savvy, intelligent, motivated women. They've since changed their group's name to the Riverside Strummers because they've invited some men to join them, but they're still wonderfully diverse and they make the best music. I truly admire them for their spirit and joy.

I love the idea that we all have hidden flames inside us, waiting to ignite.

It can happen now, or at 85.

We can keep learning forever.

Here's a question: do you know what lights you up? Have you uncovered your own beautiful mystery yet? It's inside you, waiting to shine.

If you're not sure, try this:

Be a beginner.

Beginners are allowed to be bad at stuff. That's fantastic news, right? Start and be horrible at it. It's okay. You're a beginner.

Notice what you're doing when you lose track of time.

That's what you love, so do more of it.

See what you can get away with, just for fun.

Think: *I want to see if I can...sell a painting, start a business, design a handbag.*

Ask yourself a tough question: when was the last time you learned something new?

Living with your lights ON and your motor running is the key to joy. Being a producer, not a consumer, is the key to happiness. Whatever your age, here's to finding what lights you up. It's worth thinking about and getting started.

∼

Finding Fun

What would you love to create
or learn
just for fun?

....

∼

DON'T LET ANYONE RUSH YOU

I don't know about you, but I always want to do things FAST. I jump in. I get going. I work hard. It's a strength of mine. But sometimes I wonder is it a weakness, too? Are there times when it's better for us to slow down and see what unfolds? To hold back a little?

Sometimes a project isn't a race.

Sometimes the magic is in the waiting.

The best moments, the best work, the best writing, the best idea, the best artwork...sometimes the MAGIC takes a little time.

I'm really talking to myself here—are you listening, CATHERINE?? But I guess I'm also talking to you. If you've got an idea, a special project, something new you're trying to launch, a lifestyle change, a new career, a new direction, consider this:

It takes courage to slow down. Don't let anyone rush you.

Thinking things through brings the magic.

A LIFE CHANGING QUESTION

This morning I'm writing in my pjs, too excited to shower first or get dressed because I thought of something important and I wanted to tell you. This one's a life-changer.

~

What if you told yourself
a different story
about your life?

~

WHAT IF SOME of our stories about ourselves are wrong? Maybe we've outgrown them, or they were given to us by other people. (I'm too loud. I can't sing. I'm not creative.)

Could you start a new story about yourself with those two words—what if?

What if I decided to become a morning person? What if

I was the person who plans the annual family gathering? What if I started a business this year?

I wonder what it would look like if we told ourselves a new story about our lives.

- What if I stopped being unhappy at work?
- What if I fell in love this year (with someone, or with something new)?
- What if I brushed my hair back and called my silver roots pretty?

Or maybe we could try something a lot bigger. Like this:

- What if I moved (my family) to another country?
- What if I adopted a child?
- What if hosted an orphan for four weeks through www.project143.org?
- What if I started my own business?

What if the best is yet to come?

Your New Story

Could you start a new story about yourself
with those two words—what if?
What if I were someone who...

....?

43

SHAKE UP YOUR LIFE

Now is a beautiful time to try something risky. For you, I've put together my favourite list of things to do that will automatically cause our lives to change. If you're ready to shake up your world a little, consider giving these ideas a try.

Find Expanders

Look for three people who will expand your vision of what's possible for you.

- Read about the mother who started share trading during her baby's naps.
- Learn more about the 83 year old who started painting.
- Find the novelist who also writes non-fiction.
- Follow an introvert who started a podcast.

If you want to do something new, find people who are already doing those things. You don't have to know your

Expanders personally—you can watch them online, read about them, whatever—but their job is to enlarge your world. I'll give you an example: one of my Expanders is Liz Gilbert. She's the person who lets me know I can be a fiction and non-fiction author. Though I'm not likely to be Liz's new best friend and may have a different level of success, I can learn from Liz and hold her up as an example of what's possible for me. She's doing it, so I can, too.

Learn something new.

It's amazing how simple this is and how it will help us feel better. What new skill are you interested in learning? Instead of scrolling or reading news, watch a How To video on YouTube. Here's a fun list:

- Make kombucha
- Do a cartwheel
- Wrap grocery store flowers like a florist
- Pack a suitcase
- Play chess
- Bake sourdough bread
- Take better photos
- Memorise a poem
- Trim your own fringe

Surprise Yourself.

This month, do at least one surprising thing. Change your hair (style? colour?). Take a class. Write the lyrics to a song. Buy yourself a surprising present (A baseball glove? A negligee? A goldfish?) Just do one thing, anything, that is *not you*.

Promise me, please, and see what happens.

Why?

Because the world is filled with amazing-ness, and though our neural pathways love what is the same, you deserve the surprise and wonder and joy of doing something new.

∾

Inspire Someone

If you did something new,
who would be excited for you?
Write their name here:

....

(Our growth inspires the people we love.)

∾

44

PEOPLE PLEASING

When I've had a big week, I have to admit that I get a little weary. You too? For me, there are kids and work and people—people to love and help and celebrate and reassure. It's all good. And it's tiring. Before I help too much, or work too hard, I try to think about what I've agreed to do, and how I'm acting. What is my motivation? Is it something I truly want to do, or am I performing a role out of a sense of obligation?

Am I saying *yes* to others, but *no* to myself?

For people pleasers everywhere, this message is huge: we need to know what our job is, and what it isn't. Christine Hassler, author of *Expectation Hangover* and coach at christinehassler.com, posted this on Instagram:

Not my job:

- Fix or save people
- Be liked
- Do it all

- Please everyone

My job:

- Love people
- Be authentic
- Take the next step
- Give myself time to breathe and think

It's so important to get this straight! If we do what we're called to do, and drop what we're not, we have more energy for what matters.

One of my favourite lines from my thriller, *Love Lie Repeat*, is when the anti-hero, Annie, is confronted by her friends. She's a dangerous young woman, full of power and rage, but with a fierce loyalty, too. Her friends tell her this:

It's not your job to rescue us so that we keep on loving you.

Ouch! Yes. We need to know what our job is — and what it isn't.

∼

What's NOT Your Job Right Now?

Is there something (someone)
you don't need to carry?

....

∼

45

YOU GET TO CHOOSE

Mental health workouts are as tough as going to the gym, but we all need to do it. The first step is to wake up, become aware, know that we can choose our thoughts—no matter what happens to us.

This is what it's like to be a grown-up.

And it all starts with our ability to choose.

You get to choose to practice or not. To stay the course or give up. To be positive in the face of risk. To love, and weed out your own bitter roots.

You get to choose every day.

So do I.

And sometimes, yes, it's tough to rise above the noise of our own brains and do the internal work necessary to keep our minds and spirits healthy.

No matter what happens, no matter what the circumstance, we can choose our thoughts, then generate better feelings. I love this quote from @yung_pueblo that I saw on Instagram. It made me laugh at my own crazy brain:

Why spend time building inner peace?

Because controlling the world around you
is not always an option.

He is so right. Controlling the world is not an option. But all of us have the ability to start with ourselves.

- Choose better thoughts.
- Choose kindness (especially toward ourselves).
- Choose to have more fun—and to be more fun.

Maybe it's time to give that a try.

46

ARE YOU AN ASKER OR A GUESSER?

A couple of years ago, I had a beautiful lesson in seeing someone ask, and by asking upfront, my friend ensured that she would get exactly what she needed.

Here's the story.

A woman I admire named Julia—auburn hair, smart-as-a-whip, truly beautiful—joined a video conference call. She was in the middle of a tough breakup and simply asked for what she needed:

> "What I need you to do," Julia said, "is give me some love and good vibes and distraction. I *don't* want to talk about the end of my relationship."

For me, that was WOW.

So brave.

So smart.

We can ask for what we need upfront, and most of the time people are grateful to know how to support us. It's like handing someone a detailed road map during a difficult situation and saying—please, can you respond this way?

- "I need to tell you something. I'm hoping you can give me some encouragement and support."
- "I have important news to share and I want you to be happy for me."
- "Could you reassure me? I'm feeling terrible."

Fear of rejection is the greatest human fear. Asking—for some of us—is incredibly hard. Like anything else (from push-ups to pirouettes) we get better with practise. If we ask for what we need, we make life so much easier for the people around us.

They don't have to guess.

We don't have to guess.

But we do have to be brave and ask. In every way, it's so much better than guessing.

Asking makes us aware of what we need (and sometimes we skip right over this step). It requires us to trust that other people are essentially good and want to help. Guessing grinds our gears and invites Worry in for a sleepover. Why guess when we don't have to?

∾

Asking For It

Just ask for what you need.
Start being brave with your life.
Even if you're not ready, you're ready.

∾

47

BE THE BOSS OF YOUR BRAIN

I t was incredibly freeing to learn that I was the boss of my own brain. If I woke up miserable, I didn't have to stay that way or ride it out until I happened to feel better.

I could choose better thoughts.

If I had an ingrained habit of being bitter, or jealous or small, I could choose to be forgiving or kind or expansive. I didn't have to be a slot car stuck to a track, driving around in circles.

∼

I am the CEO of my brain.
My thoughts are the employees.

∼

SEPARATING our Self from our Thoughts takes us one step closer to feeling better, but surprisingly, it's an idea that so many people don't know. And we're only now starting to teach our kids these important basics of consciousness.

We are not our thoughts. We can watch our thoughts come and go, and ultimately, we can choose what to think.

As a culture, we are pretty good at working hard and hustling. We're often good at ignoring how we feel and "just getting on with it." If we understand the simple truth that we can pause and be the boss of our brains—that we can choose better thoughts any time we want—we'll live happier lives.

When rowing season would roll around again in our household (along with those 4:30am mid-week alarms!), it reminded me why we need to choose our thoughts. A 4:30am start can be horrible. Or it can be worth it. We get to choose.

My husband told me that when Canadian naval officers rowed whalers, with six midshipmen to a boat, they were taught to focus with this phrase:

Stroke, stroke, eyes in the boat.

Focus is important.
But even more important is setting the right course first.

~

Be The Boss Of Your Own Brain

Choose 'better feeling' thoughts.
You can start anytime.
Even right now.

~

48

COMPLAINING

Gary Vaynerchuk is tough and inspirational, too. You can find him at garyvaynerchuk.com. He has some fairly direct words to say about entitlement and the kinds of excuses we allow ourselves to believe. He reminds us that if we've ever dropped $4 for a cup of coffee, we're more entitled than a huge majority of the world, and we have the resources to get moving.

No excuses.

This is a lesson I need to remember. It's been my goal this year to stop complaining and start doing—to shift from the *thinking about it* to the *doing something about it*. You're holding the result in your hands: *The 10 Minute Fix*.

Gary says this:

Complaining has a Return On Investment of zero. Always.

He's right. As much as I love to cling to the mental crutch of a good long whinge with a girlfriend, complaining accomplishes absolutely zero. Appreciation followed by action gets us further every time.

Here's what Gary Vee taught me to do:

- When things get tough and I want to complain, I tell myself that if I'm not ready to act, I can at least focus on appreciation.
- I stop.
- Look around myself (literally).
- Appreciate the things I see and have.

Fresh air, clean drinking water, having a mobile phone and a place to sleep. My kitchen table, a dog healthy enough that I have to walk her every day, a warm blanket on my bed, family who have left a sink full of dishes. A dishwasher to fill. You get what I mean.

When I'm tempted to descend into grinding over the same thoughts repeatedly, I consider Gary's tough love.

Then I take one baby step forward, and start the thing I don't want to do.

Remember the 10 Minute Fix? Set the timer and begin.

∼

The 10 Minute Fix

We can do *anything* for ten minutes.
Complaining has a
Return on Investment
of zero. Always.

∼

49

BE 'THE ONE' FOR SOMEONE

G olden Jubilee Park—that's where I took a photo
of an echidna. Echidnas are hilarious, and it
made me laugh so much. Every time I tried to
snap a photo, he'd bury his head in the leaves.

Up, down, up, down...you'd swear he was hiding from my
camera. The echidna could have been a character in an
animated Disney movie.

Makes me think of how we all live—sometimes we're
brave, sometimes we feel like burying our heads and just
being incognito for a while.

It's been a busy week for me, full of stepping out into the
unknown, pushing my own boundaries and then pulling
back.

Up, down, up, down.

Do you do this? Forge ahead with a new plan, and then
fall back? Charge, then wait? Get fired up, and then feel
overwhelmed with despair?

It's easy to wonder if we're making any lasting impact at
all. That's why I love Marisa Peer, an incredible British ther-

apist. You can find Marisa's work at marisapeer.com. In a video clip I watched recently, Marisa said this:

> If one person on the planet breathes easier because of you,
> your life has meaning and purpose.

I love the notion of making just one person breathe easier. It seems do-able. While we hustle and strive and build and grow, we can remember that our legacy can be very simple.

One act of kindness.

One heart we've loved.

One person changed: we can all do that.

∼

Be 'The One' For Someone

Who is *your* person on the planet
that breathes easier because of you?
Honour them here.
Write their name.

....

∼

50

MOTHERS AND FATHERS

S ome people have wonderful fathers. Some people have incredible mothers. Some people get a mix of that. Our relationships with our parents are complicated, of course. There is no way to explain to someone who doesn't share our history just how beautiful—or painful—the notion of *father* or *mother* can be.

One thing I do know, though, is that for most of us, we outlive our parents. And that means something important.

~

We get to choose which memories to keep,
and which to throw away.

~

WE HAVE the freedom to choose what we think about. Whether it's about our fathers, mothers, children, even about ourselves: we can choose our memories.

Sometimes it's good to let them go.

I remember a story my sister told me. She was a solo parent working full time as a primary school teacher, and on this particular day there was a big book fair in the gym at her school. Her son was in year one, only six years old. She remembers Teddy standing at her classroom door after school, asking to go to the book fair, but for some reason, (a staff meeting? students to care for in her classroom?) my sister couldn't leave to take him and she had to say no. She cried when she told me the story. She said she never forgot —as a teacher, a solo parent, a mum—what it was like to do an excellent job of taking care of everyone else's kids while her own stood at the door, waiting.

But here's the thing: when Ted was all grown, she asked him this: "Do you remember the day when I couldn't take you to the book fair?"

His answer?

A shrug. "Mom, relax. It was fine."

Oh, our memories of family, of fathers and mothers, of successes, of mistakes! Maybe it's time to let it go.

Let It Go

Sometimes we cling senselessly to our own pain.
We get to choose which memories to keep replaying
and which to throw away.

51

THE TRUTH ABOUT STICKS

Here's what I wish I knew when I was young. Every choice comes with consequences, and though you can't always see those consequences, like it or not, they will exist. And you will have to deal with them. It's the lesson of the stick.

- Choose to think miserable thoughts?
  Consequence: unhappiness.
- Choose to stay up all night and party?
  Consequence: the next morning.
- Choose to immigrate? Consequence: excitement, fun...and your life will change forever.

~

You pick up one end of the stick,
you pick up the other.

~

IT's a hard lesson to absorb. We get so enticed by one end of the stick that sometimes we don't bother thinking it through.

Now that I'm a mother, I'm trying to teach this lesson to my sons. I hope they're learning, but their lives are their own, and each of us walks a separate path.

~

The Lesson Of The Stick

Action. Consequence.
Two ends of the same stick.

(You pick up one end of the stick,
you pick up the other.)

~

52

IS IT TIME TO REST?

J ust this week, making school lunches, I was reminded of rest while I sawed away at a tomato with a dull knife. I was in a hurry and I just wanted the job done. So I kept going. When this knife was new, it was fab. It used to work brilliantly. Then, not.

Saw, saw, saw.

I was saving time! Getting on to the next thing! Powering through.

But I wasn't.

So I took a second, found the knife sharpener my sister bought me when I visited her in Phoenix, and sharpened my knife. Such a simple tool, such an inexpensive fix, such a huge result.

Slice!

Relief.

Nearly thirty years ago, Steven Covey wrote about sharpening the saw in 7 *Habits of Highly Effective People*. The lesson has been around forever. So why do we forget it?

Why do we forget to rest?

It's always faster to pause, to rest, to sharpen your (metaphorical) saw and start again.

I have to remind myself a million times: rest helps me go faster. Rest recalibrates my creativity and—frankly—makes me a much nicer family member to be around.

Nobody loves a martyr, even one who gets the job done.

So for me, this weekend is all about rest.

And a bit of chocolate.

And family, peace, renewal.

~

Nobody Loves A Martyr

Remember: sharpen the saw!

~

53

BIG MISTAKES

S ome of you will know me personally, and many of you won't. So I thought I'd share a little of my story, including what I regret and why. My big mistakes might resonate with you; if you've lived a full life, I know you've made your own.

Here are mine, in no particular order.

People pleasing.

Oh, I could write a book on this. If I could name my biggest regret it would be that I spent a lot of time doing what other people expected of me. People-pleasing is exhausting. It's not a great way to live.

Want a few concrete examples? Getting married when I knew it was the wrong thing to do, saying yes to work opportunities I knew I didn't love, maybe even my decision to immigrate. Yes, yes, yes...until NOPE.

Gretchen Rubin, American author and happiness guru (at gretchenrubin.com), calls this 'nope' response 'Obliger

Rebellion.' She says when people pleasers rebel, they usually chuck a hand grenade in order to stop.

(Yes, there is collateral damage.)

What am I learning to do differently? Start with the truth. That's where we all wind up anyway.

Letting fear make my decisions.

I often make quick decisions because it makes me feel less afraid. Sometimes this works out really well. I'm agile and I'm good at starting projects and finishing them. But sometimes quick decisions have resulted in a haphazard life without a plan.

I'm trying to take my time with my decision-making and not let Fear drive the car. I've learned to say this: "Whatever happens, I can handle it."

Let's face it, pretty much 100% of the time we have to handle it. And we do. And we can.

Feeling unworthy of (fill in the blank).

Feeling unworthy of love, attention, good luck, encouragement, praise.

Feeling unworthy is a lie. All of us are worthy of all good things, simply because we're human and we're trying our best, for the most part.

When we feel unworthy, we make choices that don't support us. Therapist Marisa Peer (at marisapeer.com) has led a movement to teach people to question feelings of unworthiness. Marisa suggests we write this on our bathroom mirrors — a simple fix with an incredible result:

I am enough.

Believing that people need to be like me (think like me, act like me).

It took me so many years to give people the right to their own opinions. Now, as a writer, I've taken a crash course in it. Writers deal in pitching and rejection and I've learned to see that one person's opinion is just that: their opinion. Not necessarily the right opinion, just another opinion.

I am not necessarily right. You are not necessarily right. We both think what we think. And finally, I'm okay with that.

Playing small.

A few years ago, I got to a point where I felt like a cicada about to burst through my shell. I was afraid of shining my crazy, imperfect light out in the world. I was waiting to be more capable or more accomplished or more ready or... something. But then I decided I couldn't wait any longer.

My life is half over and I want it to count. So (bravely) I'm putting it out there: my books, my creativity, my blog at LoveOurAge.com, my life, all the lessons I've learned. Love it or hate it, agree or disagree, I'm showing up. I hope you are, too. Mistakes are just lessons, after all.

∾

Two Useful Phrases To Remember

"Whatever happens, I can handle it."
"I am enough."

∾

54

YOU GET WHO YOU GET

You've probably heard the phrase we teach toddlers: "You get what you get, and you don't get upset." For me, it's more like this: "You get WHO you get, and you don't get upset."

I come from a big family—six kids, six!—and I learned pretty early on that you can't pick who you're going to gel with.

What is that all about? It's a mystery.

Some people we connect with immediately and love, love, love. Some people, nope. Often there isn't a very good reason for it.

You like who you like, and you are not for everyone.

I was reminded of this at fitness last week, when a fabulous Swedish-Aussie friend asked, "Did you like the novel, *The Handmaid's Tale*?" (By the way, the novel is quite different from the television series.)

Three of us were lined up in a row on the mats. On one side of my Swedish friend, doing mountain climbers or push-ups or some other godforsaken thing, I yelled out YES,

I LOVED IT and my sweet friend on the other side said OH, I HATED IT. We had a good laugh. Because we're both right.

The trick with everything is finding your tribe. And maybe the even bigger trick is realising that—with all the people who aren't your tribe—there's no point in getting upset. It is what it is.

You love who you love. You "get" who you get.

55

PRAISE YOURSELF

Everybody's different, but here's a thought. When was the last time you praised yourself? (Let me make you a virtual cup of tea while you curl up in a chair and think about it...) Really, it's important. Please take a second and consider it honestly. So many of us are quick to praise other people, but compliment ourselves?

Not often.

My son is lucky enough to own a 200 year old cello. As a musical instrument, it is so beautiful! His cello reminds me that it's hard to praise ourselves when we know the world is filled with expertise, beauty, success, talent.

Many musicians have loved and played this cello in the past two centuries, and some of them were brilliant. Is it any wonder that sometimes we think, *who am I?*

Everywhere we look, we see the highlight reel of people's lives. Instagram. Facebook. Twitter and Snapchat. The world is noisy. The crowd is loud. The pond is full of people who do what we do.

It's easy to overlook the good in ourselves.

But honestly, is it time for you to praise yourself a little?

When was the last time you said something heartfelt and kind about yourself?

Go on, please try it. I'm 100% sure you deserve it.

Praise Yourself

Is there anything you can praise yourself for?

(Me? I make delicious cinnamon buns.
I keep my promises to other people.)

Your turn:

....

56

WHAT WE CANNOT SEE

My beautiful neighbour Denise sent the perfect email. She wrote that she had snapped a photo from her back garden of the winter light filtering through our backyard tree. She wanted me to see it. "I thought the colours of the sunset were amazing," she wrote. "Shame it only lasted a moment!"

I love the picture so much.

And it made me think about what other people see of us —see of our lives—that we can't see.

I look at my back garden and see the pool that needs cleaning, the tiles that need repair, the grass that's over-grown. But from my neighbour's vantage point, she sees:

- Beauty
- A bare tree
- Two birds
- Pink sky

Her photo is a metaphor. Isn't it wonderful to think that other people often see the good in us?

We pick ourselves apart sometimes; we can be our own worst critics. All the while, other people might be seeing what's good.

We can all do more of this: notice what's right. Catch people—especially kids and teens—doing what's right.

Now is the perfect time to get started.

～

Throw Compliments Like Confetti

Today, please notice one simple thing that's right
about your surroundings and your people.
Kindness is free.

～

57

ARE YOU MISSING OUT?

Question for me and you. It's a tough one. Are you taking care of yourself? I am always so slack at this, and I want to get better at it. I mean, we're ALL pretty good at taking care of other people, right? We're helpful to friends, some of us care for families or elderly parents or grandchildren and the list goes on. But do we take care of ourselves? Not always.

Rob Bell, American pastor and author (at robbell.com), said these words and I think he's right:

Take good care of yourself.

Your greatest gift to anyone is that your tank is full, your heart is overflowing.

What do you need?

- Rest?
- Peace?
- Tea?
- To sleep more or move around more?

What I needed this week was more time in nature. So we drove three hours to my favourite beach and I stood and watched the sunset. Beauty and peace, that's how I take care of me.

Here's the deal: is there something you can do today to take good care of yourself? Because what your people really need—even when they're hurting, even when they're in trouble—is you, with a full tank and an overflowing heart.

Put Yourself On The List

One small thing that fills
my heart:

ASK YOURSELF

Offering questions to our own minds is often the quickest way to make a change. A question encourages our brains to slide into solution mode, instead of staying in the realm of the problem. When I feel stuck or unsure, a friend taught me to pause and ask:

How is this working in my favour?

YOU CAN APPLY this question to every situation.

I've found it's the quickest way to look for the good.

Get creative, be expansive, entertain some possibilities and figure out all the ways that this thing—whatever it is— is actually working out for you, to help you.

SNOWFLAKE-Y REASONS

When we were in school or university, we spent a lot of time learning, and now...maybe not so much. But we can learn almost anything for free. How to play guitar or dance the Mambo, juggle or knit a scarf, fix a laptop or plait hair or draw a building.

Hello, YouTube. Hello, Khan Academy. Hello, Internet.

Nonetheless, I come up with a ton of reasons why I'm a 'special snowflake' and it won't work for me.

- Too hard.
- Too busy.
- Not sure what I want to try.

But here's the truth: the quickest way to feel fantastic is to learn something new. (It can be something very small!)

The equation for feeling better, and for having more happiness in our lives looks like this:

Growth = Happiness

Whenever I need to get happier, I know it's time to wave goodbye to my own snowflake-y reasons about why I can't, and why it's too hard for me, and simply try learning something new.

As Margaret Atwood, Canadian author, mentioned that her mother liked to say:

Time to roll up your sleeves, girls!

She was a wise lady, and she's absolutely right.

~

What Would You Learn?

If you could learn anything (even something simple, like how to frost a cake like a pro, take a better selfie, choose a ripe melon) what would you like to learn?

Your turn:

....

....

~

RAMPAGE OF APPRECIATION

S ome days when I feel a little low, I do something I learned from my friend and podcaster Jess Lively (at jesslively.com). Jess suggests we get thankful. Not a new idea, I know, but it works so well and I love the new name she has for it!

~

Go on a rampage of appreciation.

~

HERE'S THE TRICK: you can't just name the basics—you have to go on a RAMPAGE and list everything you can.

It's a great word, right?

Whether you list all the things you love that are big or tiny, there is so much to appreciate. And when you do, you will feel better. Trust me. Try it now. Whisper your list out loud.

It works every time.

WHY I CHEER FOR PEOPLE

When you offer your work to the world, you have to expect that some people will like it and some won't. For me, fear of rejection lives in my head along with jealousy and scarcity. I think of them as three ugly sisters that are a little too close for comfort. It's way too easy to spiral down and let them have a food fight in my brain.

That's why I love these words from Tracee Ellis Ross, actor and daughter of Diana Ross (of the Supremes):

> I cheer for people. I was raised to believe there's enough sun for everybody.

What a spacious, generous way to think: there's enough for everyone.

Enough recognition.

Enough partners.

Enough love.

Enough resources.

We need to believe it.

FEELING BUSY?

I saw a funny desk sign that read: "PLEASE—I can only do twelve things at a time." It made me laugh. It sums up how I'm feeling lately. Productive. Excited about all the new things I'm learning. Motivated. Loving life.

Busy. Working hard.

And all with a side order of Overwhelm.

I had a chat with my friend, Kristen, and she made me feel so much better. She said this, so I am going to say it to you.

You're only HUMAN.

- All the conflicting things you're feeling now, right this second: HUMAN.
- Any burdens you might be carrying: HUMAN.
- The rushing and overwhelm: HUMAN.

Understandable.

Breathe in, breathe out.

You're only human. It's all okay.

7 Ways To Slow Down

1. Walk in nature.
2. Pour water into a pretty glass. Take a drink.
3. If you have pet, look into their eyes and say their name. Watch them love you back.
4. Single-task—the opposite of multi-tasking.
5. Allow yourself time to daydream. Imagine you, winning.
6. Step outside and look up at the night sky.
7. Before bed, lie on your back on the floor. Stretch your arms above your head. Notice how good this feels.

NOT MY CIRCUS

Do you ever find yourself wanting to help? As the youngest of six kids, I've always wanted to. I don't know why. Maybe because in big families, it's just expected. I was also a farm girl, and on farms, everyone helps. Also, I grew up in a climate where it can be -40 C in winter, so it's basically help or perish. And as a Mum, I help.

As I get older, I'm learning that helping is not always the right thing to do. Sometimes it's a smokescreen that allow us to avoid helping ourselves. Sometimes it's a lost cause, and we're throwing our energy into someone else's black hole of endless need.

So when I saw this this Polish proverb, I thought maybe it's for me. Maybe it's for you, too. Maybe we all need to learn what to pick up, and what to leave be.

～

Not my circus. Not my monkeys.

～

LET PEOPLE REMEMBER YOU

Y ou're here reading, and I'm grateful to share this
tiny Ten Minute Fix with you. It's so simple, but it
will impact the people you love forever.

I promise.

The best compliment I ever received is when my mother
told me, "You're a good mother." Every time I see yellow, I
think of her. It's her colour. On her fortieth birthday, my
Dad gave her a surprise: a yellow Volkswagon Beetle, tied up
with a bow. She has loved yellow her entire life and she
always chooses it. At 87, she wears it still.

I left home at fifteen years old for boarding school, and
for the past twenty two years my mother and I have lived on
opposite sides of the globe. Still, when I see anything yellow
—a rose, a shirt, a teapot—I think of my mum.

That's why I did the same thing. When my boys were
little, I told them this:

I love twilight.

It's the magical time of day. For me, the night sky brings safety and beauty and peace.

I used to whisper in my sons' little ears—those baby ears that look like seashells—"Always remember, twilight is my favourite time of day."

I wanted to leave my boys one part of me, no matter what: *twilight*. They'll see the night sky and remember me, just like my mother gave me *yellow*.

Have you thought of giving this gift to the people who love you? It's so important.

You can help them remember you.

You can start today.

∼

How To Help People Remember You

What is your 'twilight'? What is your 'yellow'?
Write it here so you'll remember.

....

Then share with the people you love.
(Perfect with children and also with partners—
it's the best way I know to honour love.)

∼

65

NOBODY PUTS BABY IN A CORNER

My friend shared a quick photo she snapped of her daughter. All the little girls in ballet class are dancing inside plastic hula hoops placed on the floor. But her little one? She's off in the middle of the room, twirling.

Underneath the photo, my friend wrote this caption as a nod to the final scene in the 80s movie, *Dirty Dancing*, where the heroine's family has her wedged at a table, her back to the corner of a room. Baby's blocked in, unnoticed.

SEE THE GREEN RING? That's my daughter's. Nobody puts Baby in a corner...

Oh, my lord. I laughed until I cried.

This little girl is dancing, not caring, outside her ring. She's not following the rules or giving a toss about being different. She is herself.

We all start there: free.

But things change.

As we get older, it can take courage to Be Catherine, Be

Adele, Be Marisa, Be Rita, or Sharon or Sandy or Tara or Sheila or Heather or Trish...in all our crazy glory. We do what's safe or what other people think is okay.

It can take time to figure out what we really love and be brave enough to do it.

My friend's little girl reminds me that nobody should put Baby in a corner.

The trick is not to put ourselves there.

∽

Nobody Puts Baby In A Corner

A tough question to ask ourselves
(with compassion and love):
Have I put myself in a corner?

....

∽

66

WARM HELLOS AND GOODBYES

It's ridiculous how happy it makes me that Microsoft Word has a pop-up message saying 'Welcome Back!' when I open an existing file on my laptop. All autumn, whenever I went back to make revisions to the draft of my novel, I was greeted with that message. I had a lot of hard work ahead of me and some days, my motivation was low.

Welcome Back!

It made me feel so much better. Two words, more happiness.

It makes me think that I should say this to my family when they get home.

Welcome Back!!

Gretchen Rubin, bestselling author and happiness guru (at gretchenrubin.com), suggests we should all give 'warm hellos and goodbyes.'

When the kids leave for school in the morning, a heartfelt 'See ya later.' When our partner comes home from work, a kiss hello. When a friend drops you off at your front door...a huge thank you? A smile? When you're leaving a shop with your groceries, an upbeat 'See you next time!'

Being real.

Being kind.

It's surprisingly easy to start a revolution.

Welcome Back to noticing our own lives, and how good they are (problems and all).

67

YOU'RE A WORK IN PROGRESS

Like you, I'm a work in progress. I'm doing fine and growing older. I'm achieving a few things, but falling short of my own goals on a regular basis. Worries, wrinkles, opportunities, joy.

But every day, social media tells us we're supposed to be perfect: fit and self-disciplined and techno-savvy and politically active and fashionable and Instagram-ready...with kids who achieve and a whole stack of personal victories that we trot out at parties.

Oh, and we're not supposed to age.

Yes, I do this. (It's easy)

Yes, I am this. (Also easy)

And the truth—that sometimes we're tired, that sometimes we fail (loudly, publicly), that sometimes we disappoint ourselves or are gutted by the people we love—that truth hides with all the photos we delete. Too old. Too fat! Too boring to share. That won't get any Likes.

Delete. (What would the online world look like if we shared our Deletes instead?)

I've decided that chasing perfection—in real life or online—is exhausting. So here's a thought:

What if we are already enough?

Can we make peace with ourselves, right now, as we are? I'm a work-in-progress. So are you.

A young friend asked me what I've learned from being 50, and I shared my hard-won truth. Maybe it will resonate with you.

∾

What I Learned By Age 50

We don't have to do it all, or do it perfectly.
We just have to do what we love.

∾

WHEN YOU ARRIVE AT YOUR DOOR

Here's a quick happiness habit I learned from a man who lives in Etobicoke, Ontario. I can't remember his name but I wish I could because I'd love to give him credit for this amazing idea. He said this:

> Every day when I walk through the doorway, I tell my partner about the best thing that happened to me. No exceptions. Best thing first.

Imagine how all our relationships would be if we always said the best thing first.

~

Your Front Door

We can use the doorknob as a trigger.
Touch it and remember, *best thing first*.

~

MUSCLE UP, BUTTERCUP

When I get tired, it's often because I've been stupid. I start comparing my beginnings to other people's middles. Nothing makes me so tired as comparing myself to others.

When that happened this week, I stopped and baked cookies. That makes sense, right?

It wasn't because I wanted to drown my sorrows in cookies. I baked them because—full disclosure—I bake the BEST cookies and, this week, I wanted to feel effortlessly good at something.

So: cookies. My quick fix.

But the truth is, these are not my cookies. I'm using my big sister's recipe; Sheila is an awesome baker and from her, I've learned how. I grew up watching her bake, and her cookies have been famous at my kids' school for a decade.

Isn't that what we all do, really?

We start with someone else's recipe.

We stand on the shoulders of the giants who have gone before us and figured stuff out, then we innovate and add our own secret sauce.

We all have to start somewhere.

Theodore Roosevelt very wisely said this:

Comparison is the thief of joy.

You're so right, Teddy. Even comparing beginnings with beginnings can be hard.

Time to look down and in, not up and out.

Sometimes I just have to tell myself to 'Muscle up, Buttercup' and get on with making my own stuff, in the only way I know how.

70

LISTEN TO YOUR HEART

On the days I find myself at my least happy, it's because I'm listening to the world and not to my inner wisdom. It is so easy to listen to everything outside ourselves.

Are you the same?

If you are, here's a little reminder for both of us. These are very important words from author Paulo Coelho (at Paulocoelho.com)—they make all the difference:

You will never be able to escape from your heart,
so it is better to listen to what it has to say.

— PAULO COELHO

71

FLIP IT OVER

Flip it: such a great concept! When I hear myself saying or thinking, "I don't want...," I flip to this: "What I do want is..." Sounds better, right? It feels more positive and optimistic, and the intent behind the phrase is so much more helpful.

It's amazing how well this works, and mental gymnastics are all it takes.

Flip it over.

- *What I do want* is a harmonious night of homework with two tired high schoolers.
- *What I do want* is help folding laundry and emptying the dishwasher.
- *What I do* want is a surprising, fun opportunity to come my way.

Have you dreamed up anything new for yourself lately? Have you thought about what you do want? Sometimes I get so busy, worried, or tired that I forget to dream. I just live my days.

But for everybody, even the most successful people, no matter how old or young we are, it's important to dream up new adventures.

Growth makes us happy.

Stagnation makes us feel terrible.

Is it time to say: "Wouldn't it be amazing IF...?"

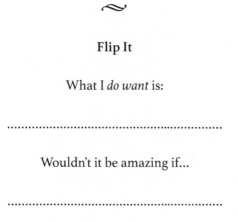

Flip It

What I *do want* is:

....

Wouldn't it be amazing if...

....

72

BE A LIGHTHOUSE

I went out for lunch with a long-time friend, Janet, and we got talking. We've known each other for nineteen years. I wish I could share her with you! She's smart and wise and works in the city. She has a mind like a steel trap and 360 degree vision and gives me the best recipes. She's a straight shooter and an invaluable friend.

She said, 'You do so many different things. Don't you feel fragmented by it all?'

Janet was right. I don't have a single message. I can't really pin myself down. Here's the highlight reel, all the good stuff:

- I'm a novelist, a non-fiction author, a picture book author and copywriter with my own business.
- I'm a blogger at Love Our Age (LoveOurAge.com)
- My first career was a role as an English teacher at a beautiful private school in Canada.
- I've done a bit of modelling recently to see what that's like for women of my age and hair colour.

- I wrote a twisty turn-y dark psychological thriller for young adults called *Love Lie Repeat* (Penguin Books) while writing a happiness blog. Dark and light at the same time!

If my list made you feel a little twinge, please let me jump in and explain. That list hits all the highlights and doesn't include times of unemployment, sadness, fear, loneliness, financial worry or the burden of school fees and a mortgage! My list is different from yours, but if we start putting ourselves on the rungs of a ladder, our lives are reduced to a superficial competition that doesn't ring true.

So let's just say this:

You've done a lot. I've done a lot. We all have.

We live in an age of 'personal brand' which makes me feel awkward and, if I'm honest, a little like rolling my eyes. I believe this whole 'personal brand' business tries to force us into a box, so we can package up and define who we are in one simple phrase. But that's not realistic.

It's taken me many years (too many!) but finally I've figured out what I want.

I want to Be Catherine, authentically.

This idea is inspired by Gretchen Rubin, happiness guru, who came up with the phrase to 'Be Gretchen' as one of her secrets of adulthood. You can find her work at gretchenrubin.com.

Be Catherine.

It's a little messy and there isn't one easy message to market. I don't fit well in a niche. Are you similar? If you've lived life, you've probably done a thing or two. Your list might be a lot longer and more grand than mine.

But here's the thing: my hope for both of us is that we haven't peaked yet. We're still growing and changing. There's still time to think about and walk towards our dreams.

If I had to be a personal brand—if I had to distill myself into a metaphor—I would try to be a lighthouse. Anne Lamott (@annelamott on Twitter), American author of my favourite book on writing, *Bird By Bird,* wrote this:

> Lighthouses don't go running all over an island
>> looking for boats to save.
>> They just stand there shining.

This is what I want to do: be a lighthouse. Stop running around the island and start shining.

Are you with me in your diverse and epic authenticity?

Then let's stand still and shine.

WHY I CELEBRATE

E ver since the boys were little, I've made small celebrations a tradition in our family. My beautiful friend, Dorothy, inspired me to do this. She blogs at Any Excuse For A Party.

In our family, if anyone has anything good happen, we celebrate. Look, it takes about fifteen minutes and it's fun. So why not?

I thought everybody did this until I met a mum at a concert. We got talking about the HSC (Higher School Certificate in Australia, basically years 11 & 12). Okay, beautiful Canadian and American readers, this is what it's all about: teens in Australia work their buns off for about 18 months straight, including over summer holidays, and I am not joking you. The last two years of high school are constant assignments, high pressure, state-wide exams, and the whole time, many teenagers are trying to get near-perfect scores to get into university. It's hard.

Anyway, this lady at the concert leaned back and told me her son just graduated from the HSC.

Me: "Oh! What are you doing to celebrate?"

Her: (Looking at me like I'm a unicorn) "Nothing. He might go out with his friends."

Me: (Inside my brain: "What the what?!?") "Okay."

In case you're wondering, this is what it looks like when we celebrate. Money doesn't matter and neither does time. It is not Instagram perfect or pricey at all:

- I set out the good crystal glasses for all four of us (yes, kids too)
- I find whatever's bubbly, usually Prosecco for adults and ginger ale for the kids
- I put on a dress, earrings, and a splash of perfume (Why do kids appreciate seeing their mothers in a dress? Little ones adore it. So cute.)
- I turn on some fun jazz
- I put some food on a fancy plate. Anything!! One time it was Maltesers (I was desperate). Or crackers and cheese, or grapes.
- I set everything on the coffee table in our living room and call in the family. Teenagers have been known to roll their eyes, but I ignore it.

Then we celebrate because I want to. As the locomotive of this family train, I also matter (not just the family, not just the whims of eye-rolling teens). If you have young kids or grandkids, this would be an easy family tradition to start. If you have teenagers, I guarantee they'll give you the side-eye, but it's so worth it.

When I yell out, "Family Celebration!" we have a way to switch on and appreciate our lives.

We make a toast "To us!" and our achievements and

share crazy stories. My husband tells truly AWFUL jokes and laughs the whole time he's telling them, which is actually kind of adorable.

Why celebrate? Why bother?

Because we're here.

Because we can.

Celebrating when things are good is awesome. And celebrating anyway in the face of fear, upset, and worry makes me brave. It reminds me to appreciate my good, crazy, unpredictable, imperfect, work-in-progress life.

How To Create An Easy Celebration

All it takes is music,
a candle or two, a few snacks and you
—calling out, "Let's celebrate!"

74

HELLO, BEAUTIFUL

Y ou deserve to hear "Hello, Beautiful!" every day. Why? Well, my guess is you've done one (or more) of the following today:

- Made a meal for someone.
- Tied little shoes.
- Wiped up the kitchen floor.
- Listened while someone shared.
- Smiled at a person you didn't know.
- Figured out a way to help.

These are the actions of a beautiful person.

Want to know why I say *Hello, Beautiful!* to myself every morning? Because I'm good at loving people. Life is short and I do my best to be kind. And yes, I am imperfect in every way. I have grey hair and wrinkles and abs of chocolate (not steel). But I don't think you give a toss about whether I do and, honestly, neither do I. I'm the kind of friend you'll have fun celebrating with; I'll hit the dance floor and never miss a chance; I will bring you chocolate cake. I'll never shame you for being fun or being you.

I am so much more than how I look. You are, too. Maybe it's time to see who you really are and say *Hello, Beautiful*.

You may think you have a little too much of this or too little of that to ever call yourself beautiful. If that's you, it's time to sing a new song. As my hilarious friend Robyn said one morning when we were both in our lycra, looking mum-ish and fifty-ish and working on getting fit:

It's okay. I'm not trying to make a living from my body.

Guess what? Me either.

Hello, Beautiful. I hope you have a wonderful day, being imperfectly, perfectly you.

HOW TO MAKE SOMETHING GOOD HAPPEN

There's a secret I want to share and—trust me—it works every time. It's very simple and absolutely anyone can do it. Here's how to make something good happen.

❧

Show up before you're ready.

❧

THAT'S IT.

Just take the leap and start something now.

Allow yourself to be imperfect.

Start today.

Be terrible at the new thing. That's okay. When you show up before you're ready, magic happens. People appear, ideas find you, opportunities open up.

Remember, it's good to call yourself a beginner. It can make you feel free.

YOUR SECRET SAUCE

A sk this question if you want to know what you're good at. It's simple, but incredibly revealing. You might even be surprised by this 10 Minute Fix.

What do people thank you for?

WHAT PEOPLE THANK you for is often the key to your secret sauce. Your answers will be what light you up—your contribution to the world.

I found it both hard and easy to come up with a list, but eventually it was this. Here's what people thank me for:

- Encouraging others
- Writing—especially when I describe how someone else feels, or when I write their 'truth'
- Celebrating—for reminding people to do it more

- Baking—my chocolate cake, macarons and more
- How I wrap gifts (I could do this all day!)

People thank me for the things that make me feel joy. The loveliest compliments I've been given throughout my life are these and I treasure them:

- My own mother told me, *You're a good mother.*
- Judy, a blog reader said, *You write like an angel.*
- On our nineteenth anniversary my husband told me, *You know why I love you? Because you make everything beautiful.*
- A friend once said, *Your light shines out of you.*

I can remember exactly where I was when I received each compliment. Without them, I may not have had the courage to write this book. It makes me realise that we all need to compliment each other more.

What do people thank you for? Do compliments hold a key to who you are? It's time to do more of what you love, so here's encouragement (if you need it): let your light shine.

∽

What Do People Thank You For?

....

....

....

∽

DON'T WHITE KNUCKLE IT

Got something hard to do? Don't white knuckle your way through. Don't grit your teeth. Try this instead.

Do something that makes you happy for ten minutes. Then dig in to the hard thing. And remember...we're talking about what makes YOU happy, not this:

- Something that makes *other people* happy.
- Something you *think* should make you feel happy.
- Something healthy that's *supposed to* make you happy (unless it really does!).

White knuckling your way through a tough task makes it worse. And guess what? You're an adult, so you get to treat yourself a little before you start.

That's one perk of growing up.

Let's use it.

GET OUT OF YOUR OWN WAY

To grow, we need to stop doing some stuff. Want to hear this magic list of four things we need to give up to get out of our own way?

1. STOP gathering information endlessly.
2. STOP saying *I don't know*.
3. STOP wasting energy on worry.
4. STOP waiting for someone else or external events to inspire, motivate or change things.

The last one is most important of all.

I don't think we're ever going to feel motivated. At least I rarely do. Most of the time, I have to decide to start, then start. (It helps if I give myself a little treat first!)

I think motivation is related to inspiration—so great when it pays you a visit, but you can't depend on it showing up for you.

If you need some help to get started, here's an unusual, 10 Minute Fix I learned recently and love. Go tiny.

~

3 Easy Ways To Go Tiny

1. Do (insert here) for 10 minutes a day.
2. Stretch in place now. (Yes, a yoga class would be better but baby steps are what we need.)
3. Watch one YouTube video about a project you want to try (planting a herb garden, customising a pair of jeans, starting your side hustle).

~

79

LET'S TALK ABOUT KIDS

Help me! Parenting can be hard. A few years ago when I was struggling, I asked my friend, Claire, for some wisdom. Claire is a business and life coach at Authentic Empowerment (authenticempowerment. com.au) and she taught me an important phrase. The older my children get—and they're teens right now—the more I've learned to tell myself this:

~

That's not *my* journey. That's *his* journey.

~

MOST OF THE TIME, I want to swoop in with superior suggestions and a plan to make all the pain go away. I want to prod and question and fix everything. I'm not sure about you, but nothing is more painful than seeing your own child hurting.

Nonetheless...

We have to hold space.

We need to allow our kids to take their own journey through to the other side.

Easy to say and hard to do, but if we keep stepping in, we limit their opportunity to grow.

Instead, I take a deep breath and whisper this to myself:

I wish I could step in, but that's not my journey. That's his journey.

80

YOU CAN START OVER ANYTIME

Right now. Or tomorrow. No matter what you've done, or what you have neglected to do. This is the truth and it's such a relief.

You can start over anytime.

Start over.

Start over.

Start over.

We all have the right to as many tries as we need.

RUBY SLIPPERS

D o you remember Dorothy in *The Wizard of Oz*? We're all like her in one important way. We're already wearing the ruby slippers. We have the ability to figure things out. We have more resources than we'd like to admit. Here's a list:

- Lessons for free on the internet
- A friend or two or more
- Libraries
- Parks or streets to walk and dream in
- Shoes
- Clean water
- Fresh air
- New ideas

Although nothing is ever easy and not much unfolds the way we think it will, we are already wearing the ruby slippers that can take us home. We just need to stand up and try a few things.

Let's click our heels together and start walking.

THE TWO BEST QUESTIONS

W hen things are tough, I like to take a fresh sheet of paper and draw a line down the middle. Then I write down the two best questions, one question on each side.

~

What's working?
What isn't?

~

I MAKE TWO LISTS. So simple, I know, but for me this clarifies a lot of the craziness inside my brain and lets me look at what needs fixing. For some reason, putting my thoughts outside myself on paper truly helps.

It also gives me a list to celebrate—all those things that I tend to ignore that I do well.

I use this exercise at least a few times a month.

In case you're curious, here's the last one I did.

What's working?

- Fitness
- Making healthy lunches
- On top of supervising homework

What isn't?

- Finding time to write every day
- Date night—never plan it
- Sleep routines—in bed too late!

When I know what's wrong, I have the chance to do something about it. That's all.

Fix up what's not working.

No judging. No condemning myself for what is happening. No wasting time. Just two simple questions to get myself back on track.

If you've ever wondered what's really bothering you, try the Two Questions. The truth will land like a butterfly on your 'What's NOT working' list. It's simple, but it works.

∾

What's Working?

....

....

....

....

What Isn't Working?

....

....

....

....

83

EMBRACE DISCOMFORT

Apparently, all of us have a fantasy profession. Have you ever thought about it? About what you'd be if only? Mine is kind of surprising. Secretly, I would love to be an orthodontist.

Don't get me wrong—I don't actually want to become an orthodontist. First up: science, which always makes me think, 'Do I care?' Then there are the years of uni. But ever since I had my own adult braces, and walked two sons through their braces as well, I have become strangely intrigued by orthodontics.

I mean, braces are MAGICAL.

You get a beautiful result and you don't have to try. You don't have to run or stop eating cookies or practise your serve or learn to whip up a souffle; you just put up with the braces, go to a zillion appointments, wait two years and voila...all better.

So anyway, I've found out that most things in life do not work like braces.

To get a different result, you have to actively seek out discomfort. You have to do stuff. New stuff. Hard stuff. And keep on doing it. It's not as easy as letting something hard be done to you.

It's such a bummer.

Who wants to be brave? Awkward? Fearful? Who wants to run up a hill, then another one? (Okay, sporty people do, but generally I feel the same way about sports as I do about science. My husband and sons and trainer all tell me that sporty people already know the lesson about Discomfort. They learned it at training. Go figure.)

I've finally realised there is a weird correlation between how uncomfortable you can stand being and how much you achieve. We put off being uncomfortable, hoping we can make up for it tomorrow.

We foolishly believe that 'later' there will be more time than in our entire pasts.

But there is never going to be more time. We have to do it now.

Being scared is okay. Feeling exposed is okay. Feeling stupid, with a side order of ridiculous, is okay.

Seeking comfort instead of taking a shot at the basket will keep us stuck. Forever.

My son's amazing orthodontist, Alannah, said something to me once when we were talking about a novel I was pitching. I told her I felt nervous now that my manuscript was being read by five amazing publishers. (Okay, nervous and excited. Nervous and hopeful. Nervous and grateful.)

What if it didn't work out?

What if I had to tell people I tried and failed?

In her delicious Scottish accent, Alannah said to me:

If you don't take a chance, you don't stand a chance.

Discomfort is a good thing. It's the only way to get somewhere you've never been. And if you take small enough steps, anyone can run up a hill.

~

Embrace Discomfort

How uncomfortable we're willing to feel
is directly related
to how much we achieve.

~

84

THE GIFT OF MAKING A DECISION

Today I went shopping. Have you ever noticed that it can be fun and completely overwhelming, all at the same time? So much choice. Sometimes too much choice.

Then I listened to a podcast by Brooke Castillo, a coach and owner of The Life Coach School. Brooke said this:

Give yourself the gift of making a decision.

That word GIFT just stopped me cold. Because it's true. I burn through so much energy not making a decision.

I dither.

I think.

I wait.

Not over nail polish, obviously, or what to buy at the fruit and veg market, but over the big stuff.

Have you ever been there? Unable to decide because something is so important to you and you really (really) want to get it right?

For the past month, I've been working on the planning

stages for three different novels—a new young adult book, a new adult thriller, an adult contemporary novel—and driving myself crazy while I try to make the best choice of what to work on first. (Want to come over for a coffee? No? I can see why.)

But now I know what I need to do: I need to give myself the GIFT of making a decision.

Then move on.

~

Give Yourself A Gift

What about you?
What do you need to decide?

Give yourself the gift of a making a decision about...

....

~

85

DO YOU STRUGGLE WITH PERFECTIONISM?

I find it so hard to turn my perfect dreams into imperfect reality. Are you the same? Do you ever have a vision of how something will be, or look, or sound—and then you fall short in the execution? Or you don't even try to execute because you know it won't be perfect?

Yeah, that thinking will stop you.

It stopped me from writing for *thirty years*, and then I decided the pain of staying locked inside myself was too great—and I had to act.

That's why I wrote my first novel.

And it was exciting and so much fun and also less ground-breaking and earth-shattering than I wanted it to be. I didn't get featured on celebrity book clubs. (Yes, every author wants to be chosen by Reese Witherspoon!).

I haven't had a movie deal (yet!).

But I fulfilled a dream of mine. I learned so much. I changed. I became something I always wanted to be. I connected with readers who told me my book made a differ-ence. I spoke at high schools and coached dozens of girls through some challenging ideas about perfection and self-worth. And I learned this:

Even if your work is imperfect, it is still worth it.

I know it is from experience.

Allow yourself to be a beginner and start. Baby steps are all it takes. Remember the 10 Minute Fix?

You can do anything for ten minutes. You can take the first step towards your dream.

86

FIGURE-IT-OUT-ITUDE

A ndrea Hanson is a coach who also lives with a diagnosis of Multiple Sclerosis. If you're interested in learning more, you can find Andrea online at andreahansoncoaching.com. I heard her speak on a podcast; she was brilliant, and she said this:

I pride myself on my street smarts and figureitoutitude.

Oh, how I love that word!

Figureitoutitude. I love it so much I wish I'd thought of it.

It's what I need:

- Resilience.
- Tenacity.
- The ability to sit down and make a list and work out where to start.
- Belief that it's doable if I take baby steps.

Figureitoutitude is connected to confidence, and confidence is something we have to grow, step by step.

We gain it by doing.

The first step is admitting what we don't know (even if it's overwhelming). Then we can start to learn.

We'd all like to begin near the top, but most of us don't. Most of us start a lot closer to the bottom. It's an irritating cliche but it's true:

Everyone has to start somewhere.

Everyone *has* started somewhere.

I don't follow celebrity news, but once I read that Justin Bieber asked Selena Gomez to take off her high heels because he was embarrassed about his height. Selena told him, "You're short. Embrace it."

Poor old Justin. Really, I do feel for him. It's a big ask, isn't it, to embrace reality? It's hard for everyone.

We all have to embrace our doubt and carry on anyway.

Figureitoutitude.

Such a great word. Maybe with whatever you're facing (or embracing) in your life, you need more of it too.

∾

Embrace It

Is there something you need to figure out?

∾

BAD NEWS

A friend had to deal with some bad news three weeks ago. She drove on a winter highway in the dark and the wind to sit in a hospital and watch someone she loved go through the most terrible pain.

When bad (and very bad) things happen, what can we do? Often very little but this: love the person in front of us.

No matter how much we want to, we can't erase horrible circumstances or make them un-happen. Sometimes we can't even reach the person who is hurting. But we can love the person right in front of us, and the next one, and the next one and never stop. Spread love. It's all we can do. Sometimes it has to be enough.

~

What We *Can* Do When Something Goes Wrong

Love the person in front of us.

~

ARGUING WITH REALITY

B yron Katie, author and teacher at thework.com says that when we argue with reality, we lose—every time. She's right. We can argue with our past. We can argue with the results of our choices. We can argue with other people's decisions. We can argue with our circumstances or what was 'done to us.'

But we will lose. Every time.

What would be better? Maybe we should tell ourselves a different story, one that sounds more like this:

"I'm doing the best I can, and I'm allowed to move on."

It's easier than arguing, and so much more effective.

❧

Let's Win

When we argue with reality,
we lose 100% of the time.

❧

HOW OLD ARE YOU?

At the beach recently, I stopped to chat to a couple of mums. You need to know an important detail about me: I am young (early fifties) and I have silver grey hair. I stopped colouring it at 48. It's my thing, being 'age positive' and loving the middle of my life, and I blog about it at LoveOurAge.com.

The mums had those incredible jogging strollers, two kids in each. They were super-fit, energetic, and looked fantastic. They were Aussie beach babes, truly.

"Those strollers are amazing," I said. "It would have been great to have had something similar when I had my kids."

The blonde one with a perky ponytail shook her head and said, "I can only imagine. It must have been REALLY HARD BACK THEN."

Dead silence. Ahem.

I don't think of myself as middle-aged, even if I am—and even if I look it. Just fifteen years ago, I was in the delivery room having my second baby. And I'm starting a new career now as an author, in the middle of my life.

There's something fun about being a late bloomer, and not giving a toss that you are. I'm like the headmaster at my son's school who tells the boys:

You don't want to peak at 16.
    I haven't peaked yet, and I'm 70.

When my Mum turned 80, I asked her, "How old do you feel?"

She said, "About 35. I'm always shocked when I look at my own face in the mirror."

Me too. I'm energetic and healthy and I don't feel older than mid-thirties. I wonder if all of us hit 35 and stop. I wonder if we all stay there. Maybe the person on the scooter or in the walking frame is really only 35 inside.

～

Fun! How Old Do You *Feel*?

How old are you? ....

How old do you feel? ....

My numbers are 53 and 35.

～

90

YOU ARE NOT FOR EVERYONE

W hy is this such a hard lesson to learn? Truly, it's taken me half a lifetime to get there. Dita Von Teese, American burlesque dancer, businesswoman, fashion designer, singer, vedette, model and actor says this:

> You can be a delicious, ripe peach
>> and there will still be people in the world
>> who hate peaches.

She's right.

We are all so incredibly different: peaches or pears or apples or plums. Grapes or kumquats. Watermelon, lemon, papaya, kiwi.

Sour, sweet, unique.

You may hate my work (or me). You may love my work (or me). I'm okay with that.

I've finally grown up enough to give people the right to their own opinions. It's truly such a relief. What other people think of us is really about them—their preferences, their experiences, their minds, their lives.

I am not for everyone.
Neither are you.

Want peace? Remember peaches.
Some people love them. And some don't.

91

SHOWING UP FOR OURSELVES

Before we switched to training together in our simple garage-gym, my husband and I used to train in the park with a bootcamp group. We had to move out of our house for a couple of weeks while our timber floors were being replaced, and I said I wouldn't be at fitness class but I would 'try to work out.'

Think about the lack of energy behind that.

I'll try to exercise.

- I'll try means I can quit anytime if I need to.
- I'll try means I'll sort of try, if it's convenient.
- I'll try isn't a commitment.

Try is an escape hatch I was building for myself. I'll try to exercise, but it might be too hot or cold, windy or wet. I'll try to make it, but I might be too busy or late, tied up with work or stressed. I'll try, but I probably won't. I'm just saying I'll try.

What if we replace *try* with *will*?

I will exercise twice a week, even if it's for ten minutes.

Say it to yourself; the difference is incredible. The energy behind 'I will' feels so much stronger than 'I'll try.' I will means you're showing up for yourself and keeping a promise to yourself. It means you can trust yourself to deliver. Will is a commitment. Try—for me, anyway—is often a lie.

≈

7 Ways To Work Out More

1. Lower the bar.
2. Sleep in your gym gear.
3. Mark an X on a calendar when you're done.
4. Walking counts, at least a little.
5. Dance to your favourite 'guilty pleasure' song. You know which one—the embarrassing one. *Rock The Boat? Walking On Sunshine?*
6. Buy new workout gear.
7. Remember the 10 Minute Fix—yoga or push-ups, lunges or sit-ups. Set your timer for 10. Do.

≈

92

MAKING ASSUMPTIONS

D o you want to hear a funny story about making assumptions? (You do. You really do.) When my friend Margie and I were first-year teachers in our twenties, we rented a desperately cold house in British Columbia, Canada, heated by a massive, black wood burning stove in the living room. In the autumn and winter, that stove required a stream of boyfriends to feed it.

When men came to the house to pick us up for a date, we'd sweetly inquire if they would mind chopping—um—a cord of firewood so we didn't freeze. But first we'd have to collect that wood in a wheelbarrow from the owner's garage across the road. I hope I'm remembering this correctly. It was a lifetime ago.

Every darn day, we would wake up early and feed the stove. We'd stay up late to make sure there was enough wood to keep it going so we weren't cold in the night. It worried us; we talked about it constantly.

Finally, the long winter was over. It was spring. The owner of the house dropped in, frowned and said,

You girls should turn up the heat. It's freezing in here.

... and he pointed to the *thermostat* on the wall. The house had central heating, but we'd never turned it on.

Yep. That's a true story.

~

Is It Really True?

What seems 'so obviously true' to you?
Could you be making an assumption?

~

93

STOP WATERING DEAD PLANTS

You might have heard this wise piece of advice before, but it was new for me and wow, did it ever resonate. Where I saw this quote online, it was attributed to American speaker, television presenter and coach, Mel Robbins at melrobbins.com.

Stop watering dead plants.

My Canadian sister, Dar, a beautiful soul and a devoted gardener, visited me in Sydney a few years ago and we rediscovered how much we had in common. Dar explained a similar sentiment in another way. She always says this:

I'm going to drop that bag of rocks.

It's a powerful image.
How hard would it be to carry a bag of rocks? Literally, so hard. Figuratively, also hard. Why carry it, that big problem, the situation that hurts us so deeply, the wound from

the past that we can't change? Why spend time watering or carrying something that won't respond to our energy?

- The relationship is over.
- The deal didn't go through.
- The past happened.

When I was twenty-eight, I decided—almost out of spite —that when bad things happened to me, I would respond by aggressively pouring some good into the world. At the time, it was my way of giving a grand 'Get lost!' to whomever or whatever caused the problem. Even though I'm a little more mature now, I still do this.

Here's how it works: the good I pour into the world doesn't have to be equal in value or size. (For example, my car door gets scratched; I bake a surprise chocolate cake for my neighbour.) Replacing the bad with some good, with something I have control over, always makes me feel better.

Whatever disappointment you're facing, small or scary, consider pouring some good back into the world. You'll drop the rocks, travel lighter, and feel more in control.

∾

A List Of Rocks I'm Dropping

1. ....

2. ....

3. ....

∾

94

THICK SKINNED

A story for you: when I took my first (and only) novel writing class, we had to submit a chapter for workshopping. What happens, you ask? Everyone comments on your work, but there are ground rules to keep it constructive. You say, "I enjoyed X" and "I have a question about Y."

Fine. I was nervous, but confident. I reminded myself of my degrees (two), my career as an English teacher (a decade) and my copywriting business (fifteen years of writing many hours every day).

But there was one small detail: I didn't know how to write a novel. I was a complete beginner.

Anyway, my turn came. And a guy with a novel that was pretty bad—as in, he submitted 30 single-spaced pages of awful science fiction about a planet you actually hoped would implode, killing everyone dead just so you could stop reading the manuscript—this guy stood up, waved my pages and yelled:

"I JUST DON'T GET IT! I DON'T GET ANY OF IT."

The room was silent. Nobody spoke.

He didn't play by the rules.

I was so shocked that I laughed—out of nervousness and mortification.

It took me a few days to get over what he said, even though I knew he was wrong. Have you ever been there? Our hearts keep getting involved even though our heads know better.

It's hard to let our heads take over, sew a few clumsy stitches into that red pumping thing in our chests and keep on working. But I did. And guess what? A publisher loved my novel, shared it around his office, and invited me to submit the finished book. That manuscript led me to write another book, *Love Lie Repeat*, published by Penguin Books —and I still hope to sign a publishing deal on that first manuscript soon. Fingers crossed.

We'll see.

But I know one thing for sure: my heart's a lot tougher than it was before I started.

My dear high school friend, Heather, has a father who said something very wise. I live by it still.

If you remember nothing else from *The 10 Minute Fix*, remember this.

～

The Most Important Lesson in *The 10 Minute Fix*

You can't start younger.
You can't start smarter, either.
You just have to start where you are.

～

95

SING A NEW SONG, CHIQUITITA

"I love playing poker on Family Night," my son who was eleven at the time said. (This may mean you shouldn't take my advice, but I have a good story for you. I promise.)

When we play poker or Monopoly or Scrabble, I like to have fun. I sing, break out the drinks and table dance—you know, where your shoulders dance but your butt stays in the chair? Please say you do it, too. The boys, including my husband, find me highly irritating. But I rock on.

During our last poker night, I found ABBA *Solid Gold* on Spotify and sang all fourteen verses of 'Chiquitita.'

I was loud and slightly off-key.

The boys' eyes rolled so far back in their sockets they could have been extras in a horror movie. My teenage son, a musician, looked like he was in physical pain. But I LOVE singing that song. Remember the lyrics about sorrow and how it makes us feel like we're in chains?

Oh, ABBA. It's so true: people everywhere are enchained by sadness. Too tired to dream. No energy to start something new. Scared to try again.

Life hands us trouble and it's easy to sling on the chains.

- We hide in plain view.
- We keep ourselves small.
- We definitely stop dancing.

And we forget we have a choice. We're enchained by our own sorrow.

Hey!!

You can wake yourself up.

Time to sing a new song, Chiquitita.

~

Sing A New Song

A tough question, asked with love:
is it time to wake up about something?
What is it?
(or...Who is it?)

....

~

96

HOW TO GET UNSTUCK

You know the feeling, right? Being stuck is an ugly cocktail of confusion, doubt and worry with a big dash of lack of motivation. For the past couple of months, this was my reality—and I needed to get through to the other side. Just recently I have. So if you find yourself treading water, these tips might help.

Admit you're afraid.

Being stuck is always about fear, so announce that you're afraid. Be honest about it. Talk to your fear. Thank it for being there and for trying to protect you. Our fear can give us a beautiful opportunity to take a little time and sort out our thoughts.

Zig where you used to zag.

If you get up early, try sleeping in a little. If you run, try doing a massive walk instead. Get a coffee from a different cafe. Listen to country instead of pop, or jazz instead of classical. Drive a different route.

Practice being hopeful.

Oh, this is big.

Sometimes when I'm stuck, though I know I should be grateful, I really want to whack the person who reminds me to count my blessings. Other times, I can use a Rampage of Appreciation and get on track.

When I don't want to be grateful, I try to practise being hopeful instead.

∼

Practise Being Hopeful

Fill yourself with hope.
What is the *best* that can happen?

1. ....

2. ....

3. ....

∼

BITTERSWEET

"Everything blooms in autumn in Sydney," I called out to a fellow dog-walker yesterday. The trees were gorgeous, loaded with white and purple blossoms. So was the ground.

"Yes, and it's such a mess to clean up," she said.

She was right.

And I'm right.

There are beautiful messy blossoms everywhere.

It made me think—two people can look at exactly the same circumstance and see a different truth. Every moment, we get to choose bitter or sweet.

Are we blessed or burdened? Are we overcoming a problem, or stuck in it? Are the blossoms beautiful or just another mess?

Life is bittersweet.

What I know is this: I can't control circumstances. Blossoms will fall. But I have 100% control over the story I tell myself about them.

I make myself happier when I choose sweet.

ABOUT YOUR DREAMS

Yes, the pond is crowded. Fish teem under the surface. Ducks float, their unseen feet frantically paddling. The water is alive with snails and frogs and mozzies, plants, weeds and tadpoles...algae, slime and microscopic life too miniscule to see.

This pond is too full, you think. Crammed! Claustrophobic! And you're right. Every pond is full.

- There are millions of painters. But there's only one you, painting.
- There are millions of songwriters. But there's only one you, composing.
- There are millions of authors. But there's only one you, writing. Or one me.

I learned this lesson when I finished my first novel. For less than $20, I printed the A4 draft at Officeworks and had it ring bound. Then I sat on our patio in the sunshine and read it. And with every page I realised: this came from me. It's mine. Only I could have arranged these words in this order, described love in this way, placed this quotation from *Jane Eyre* beside that one from *The Count of Monte Cristo*, put this sonata in the hands of that teenage boy who is a cellist, made this girl run.

Only I could have built this book.

Not the thousands of writers.

Only me.

That's why there's room for all of us to keep creating. Because yes, in every pursuit, there are thousands...millions even. But only one you. And only one me.

It's time to celebrate yourself. (And start working.)

❧

Don't Give Up

Don't let someone
who has given up on their dreams
talk you out of yours.

❧

99

WAITING FOR PERFECTION

*Z*ero forward momentum. Standing still and hoping to magically (somehow?) learn to do the thing, without actually starting. Have you ever done this —waited for perfection?

I spent about three decades waiting. I wasn't good enough at writing, and so I waited to write. Instead, I imagined stories every minute of the day. When I was in one place, I was imagining someplace else. I strode across the grounds of an ancestral home, not the gravel schoolyard. I rode a white mare, not an orange banana bike. I built a kingdom in the empty pastures of my prairie home, filled with dragons and witches and princes and...me.

And I grew up, exactly like Thoreau warns...with quiet desperation. With the song still in me.

As an adult, I judged everyone I met, stored their idiosyncrasies, turned people into characters (Evil Queen! Loyal Friend! Cheating Prince!) rather than letting them be human or paradoxical or flawed.

My boyfriends called me critical.

Finally, in my forties, a lightning bolt struck. The imagining and evaluating and criticising meant I was a writer; I just hadn't started the Writing Down part. And so I did that, every day for four months. I wrote stuff down.

At the end of four months I had a draft of a novel. Not too long, just 80,000 words, but a whole complete novel, with a beginning and an end and characters and plot and tension. A world on paper. A miracle.

I barely knew what I was doing, even though I'd read thousands of books. And had a graduate degree in Literature. And taught English classes for a decade. And had my own copywriting business for fifteen years.

Writing a novel when you've read one is like sewing a wedding dress just because you've worn one: it comes out wonky. But out it comes. And then the delicious part starts: you get to revise it. Fix it! Renovate! Do an extreme makeover. For me, revision is heaven on earth because it allows us to get better. Revision gives us second chances.

Margaret Atwood is a writer I fell in love with when I was fourteen. She sent me a letter about *Love Lie Repeat* and I framed it for my study wall. She says this:

If I waited for perfection, I would never write a word.

∿

Inspire Yourself

What wonky, imperfect thing
are you waiting to create?

....

∿

100

FINALLY AND FIRST, BACK YOURSELF

E very day, I promise to listen to my heart before I consider the opinions of the world. I vow to have my own back, no matter what. It's been a journey to get here, but I believe there's an internal compass waiting to guide us all if we get still and listen.

If I could open the door to my study and show you where I write, you'd see a white desk, a red wooden heart decoration draped over white timber blinds, and on the wall a hand-lettered poster of Elizabeth Gilbert's words:

∾

"Consider the radical notion
that you're doing things right."

∾

INSTEAD OF ANALYSING ALL the reasons you could be wrong, how about assuming you're right?

You're learning exactly what you're meant to learn.

You're doing better than you think you are.
You just need to *keep going*.
Please back yourself—no matter what. Say you will.

～

All The Stars

If you loved *The 10 Minute Fix*,
please review it—give it all the stars
you think it deserves,
and gift a copy to a friend.
Thank you.

～

MINING DIAMONDS

Afterword

Do you believe reading connects us? I do. I'm thinking of you now, on an autumn Wednesday afternoon at 5:30, as I write at my kitchen table while the daylight wanes.

My dream is to give you a small book that will help you feel better, a book that earns a permanent spot on your bedside table. I hope you write in it and fold the corners down on pages you enjoy, so you can read them again.

100 simple ways to feel better now.

Right now.

Not after you create a new habit, or work at it, or transform yourself into some Future You who is supposed to have more willpower and skills than you do today.

Nope.

I want you to feel encouraged when you need it. I want to meet you where you *are* with a practical 10 Minute Fix.

I honour you here, in these pages: you're showing up, daring to start, getting up again when things don't work out, shining your light in the world.

I wish I could invite you to a party tonight at our home in Sydney! I wish I could introduce you to each other and hear the buzz and jangle of your laughter! I'd raise my glass and say thank you for seeing the world through my eyes.

If you need a final sign from this book, let it be this:

You are enough, just as you are.
    You can start now, or begin again.

We're all in this together, learning lessons we can share —each one of us mining diamonds in our own backyard.

Thank you for reading.

I believe in you.

I appreciate you.

I do.

∽

ACKNOWLEDGEMENTS

To my wise family and friends, thank you.

Adele Poier, for encouraging me to write this book. Jean McCarthy, for lighting the path. Luther, Luke and Elijah: my team, my backup, my everything. Katie Greer, best mother and friend. Sheila Eskdale, Darlene Nast, Rena Mazer: soul sisters.

Women who inspire me and lift me up: Jules Van Mil, Heather Getz, Claire Hall, Jenny Howell, Janet Anderson, Marg Hagey, Victoria Buda, Merilyn Beretta, Tara Ray, Judy Oliver, Kristen Prewitt, Sharon Cowin, Dorothy Hawes, Zoe Paraskevopoulos and Colleen Kavanaugh.

To the incredible team working with Balmoral Press, especially Kelly Weber, thank you for your agility, enthusiasm and street smarts. The best is yet to come.

To my readers and blog readers, I wish I could call you all by name.

I think of you every time I write.

～

MORE BOOKS TO LOVE!

NEW RELEASES FROM CATHERINE GREER

Small Steps Are Perfect

"Encouraging and inspiring, like warm advice from a good friend."

Paperback and ebook available on Amazon worldwide

The 10 Minute Fix Journal

"The perfect companion to *The 10 Minute Fix.*"

Available now on Amazon!

- Beautiful 214 page journal — every page is unique.
- 200 guided questions for journalling.
- 100 inspiring, practical affirmations.
- All writing prompts are based on the best-loved book, *The 10 Minute Fix.*
- Matte black cover with gorgeous blue feather (full colour).
- 6 x 9 inch (15 x 23 cm) paperback journal, lined, printed on cream paper.
- Hardcover is available in America and the U.K.

ABOUT THE AUTHOR

Catherine Greer lives in Sydney, Australia with her family. When Catherine isn't writing books, she runs Love Our Age, a lifestyle blog. *The 10 Minute Fix* is her debut non-fiction book, followed by *Small Steps Are Perfect: simple ways to find comfort & joy*. Her Young Adult thriller, *Love Lie Repeat,* was published in 2019 by Penguin Books. In 2018, she released *Jacaranda Snow*, a picture book about Australia.

Catherine holds a Bachelor of Arts (Honours) and a Master of Arts. She started her career as an English teacher at a private school on Vancouver Island, Canada. When she immigrated to Australia, Catherine launched a corporate copywriting business in Sydney. You can find Catherine online at catherinegreer.com.au, LoveOurAge.com and on Instagram @catherinegreerauthor.